BODY LANGUAGE IN 40 DAYS

JESUS ENRIQUE ROSAS

A FEW WORDS BEFORE WE BEGIN

First of all, I want to thank you for having "Body Language in 40 days" in your hands; I have done my best to make this book a complete non-verbal communication learning program.

When I started writing it in January 2011, I was feeling a bit disoriented; despite having more than 100 blog posts under my belt, I confess that the prospect of creating my first book made me quite anxious: I spent long blank sessions at the keyboard, wondering what I could offer in this volume that I had not already captured in my original blog. Obviously, presenting new information was not enough and there would have to be a purpose beyond that; an added value that would make it memorable to read. It may seem a somewhat peculiar concern, but it was something I was racking my brains over as I tried to organize the number of topics I intended to handle in those future pages. Illustrators and manipulators, microexpressions, paralanguage, persuasion, seduction, proxemics, fragments of psychology, history and anthropology, trying to spice it all up with descriptive graphics... looked a lot like a titanic task).

I've never liked to do things lightly or leave things half-finished. Things either get done right, or... get done right! This has been my motto for as long as I can remember. Even against the perfectionism I profess, I have had to accept that sometimes things can't turn out just as you imagine them, because spontaneous expression is more important than delayed perfection.

That was one of the most important lessons I learned as a blogger. One thing is what you think your readers will love... and quite another is what will really captivate them. When it comes down to it, those articles that I thought were going to fall into oblivion are the ones that practically carry the public's ovation on their shoulders, triumphant and admired. More than once I have been perplexed by this phenomenon, and it has taught me a very important lesson:

Sometimes you just have to do things as they come, with freshness and spontaneity.

The main goal of "Body Language in 40 Days" was to establish the generating concept, to specify a logical structure and to develop a particular system that would differentiate it from the rest of the books with similar themes.

What was this "something" that would set him apart?

As I went through my library analyzing book after book on kinesics, NLP, persuasion, psychology and other related subjects, I noticed a similar pattern in all of them: they were organized from the general to the particular. In most of them, the overall notions of the subject were presented first, as well as some historical references in the form of anecdotes, and then they would move on to specific topics.

The problem I saw with this system is that once the path forked like Borges' garden, it was difficult to keep up with each of those branches simultaneously. Its chapters could be viewed in any order, as each and every one was practically self-contained, each being a microcosm of knowledge. This was good and bad at the same time, since on the one hand it facilitated the subsequent review of each topic but prevented the progressive construction of knowledge.

Would there be anything wrong with that? Well... not so much. Books structured under this scheme continue to sell (and in industrial quantities!). However, as I have always said and will continue to affirm throughout this volume, body language is learned just like any other language: First, under a logical sequence of difficulty; and second, practicing daily is the only way for the knowledge to last and mature over time.

It was here that I encountered a great irony: having always professed flexibility in educational models, I would have to opt for a rigid sequence for the structure of this book in terms of the construction of learning.

That is why I approached this book as a "step-by-step" guide, as its original cover says, which would reward you for pausing every time the book indicated you to do the proposed exercises. Progress would only be possible through a sincere self-evaluation that would lead you to pronounce the words: "I am ready", unlocking your access to the next lesson.

"Don't move on to the next chapter until you've overcome the challenge of the one you're reading."

I would get a little frustrated when my first readers would tell me after just a few days that *"They couldn't put it down and loved it"*. This annoyance arose because obviously they were ignoring the instructions, which were not meant to satisfy autocratic impulses, but rather pedagogical: they are essential to give your mind and body absorb each lesson progressively.

Two years later, I decided to make a revision for the second edition. Those of you who have been with me since that August 19, 2011 when this creature came to life will see a volume with much more material than the previous one. Finally, in 2017, I decided to do the most recent content revision to make sure that the examples would not have become outdated.

And long last, ten years after the original version saw the light of day, here's the English version. Why did it take so long? I myself don't know the answer to that question...

Those of you who are reading me for the first time, know that this is the result of numerous consultations with those beloved readers who gave me the assertive indications that set the North Star to this reedition; from the inclusion of more descriptive images to the tips on each lesson, everything has been thanks to the feedback of those who, like you, decided one day to approach this reading corner and entrust me with the task of showing you the first steps in learning Body Language.

Thanks to your comments, we will all be able to continue advancing in this didactic interaction; and thanks to the dissemination of this knowledge, you will help me to continue towards our ultimate goal: To ensure that this subject is taught in schools, so children learn to use both verbal and non-verbal language and become more assertive and self-confident.

Only one thing hasn't changed: the original structure, the step-by-step learning. The recommendation to move forward only when the heart is convinced of the mastery of the current chapter. That remains unchanged. I hope that will be our bond, our union as initiates, as you continue to learn beyond these 40 days that you're about to start.

I warmly welcome you to "Body Language in 40 days". Enjoy the journey!

Jesus.

jrosas@knesix.com

To M, E, I.

INTRODUCTION

It was a particularly cold evening, near Westminster Bridge. The sky was giving way to a premature night, my perception of time disordered by recurrent wanderings through books on anthropology and psychology. Matthias, my eccentric fellow student, was palliating incipient hunger with a snack whose name was as strange as its appearance.

We hadn't spoken for an hour (and didn't really miss each other's words), as we had spent the last two weeks engaged in intense discussions on topics as varied as kinesics and the history of psychoanalysis; from the birth of language to the configuration of the human brain. Finishing our snack and slowing down a bit, my red-haired friend did his best to pull a small book out of his outer jacket pocket.

The volume was a perfect demonstration of how dirty, torn and worn a text can become. Curiosity pricked me mischievously as I wondered about its contents, but I wasn't about to break the silent streak that had accompanied us up to that moment. Trying to get a glimpse of the cover from afar, I was almost sure it was a dictionary, when suddenly...

"Voulez-vous boire quelque chose avec moi.... ce soir?"

The phrase brought me back to the moment. It was indeed a dictionary, one of those that tourists use to dive into a language with a few hours and a lot of confusion. Even though the most obvious of questions *("Are you learning French?"),* would arouse the German's sharp sarcasm, exhaustion overcame my will:

- Ah, you want to learn French?

- No.

But of course, I couldn't deserve less than that. The question was silly (and yet I asked it). Perhaps Matthias noticed my dismayed face, for he hastened to clarify:

- No, Jesus. I'm not kidding you either, although you have to admit that you would have made it very easy for me. I'm not really learning French. It doesn't interest me at all.

The cover of the book, its contents and what he just said, questioned such a statement. At the same time, I remembered his desire to visit Paris, and that he was planning to do so in the coming weekend; therefore, I did not see much sense in denying the fact. As expected, another question came up, this time a logical one:

- If you are not studying French... and if you are not interested in it at all... then.... What are you doing?

A laugh preceded the response.

- You misunderstood me. I'm literally not interested in learning French. *What I really want is to know how to talk to French women.*

This time, the laughter was mine. I thought it was an excellent idea; why learn so many grammatical and verbal rules, vocabulary and style? What Matthias wanted was the same as any bachelor visiting La Ville Lumière: to be in tune with the local females. What more could he want... Add a bottle of Champagne to the equation and that's it!

More than two decades separate us from this scene, and I have since considered it a moment of pure enlightenment. I was studying kinesics in London at the time, and the stress of the aggressive learning system was taking its toll on the fun and motivation that had initially characterized my love of body language.

The more I rationalized the process of "reading" the gestures, the more it became mechanical and even tedious. How was it possible, if a handful of months ago I claimed that I could study with such intensity for years? maybe sleeping three hours a day on a recurring basis was making me "a little" irritable?

However, after hearing Matthias' sentence, my perspective changed: I realized that it was necessary to study why we lose the ability to interpret body language at a very young age and then have such a hard time rediscovering those faculties.

As in the case of Matthias, the process is made much easier by synthesizing all the scientific background and approaching it from a practical point of view, as it is not our intention to become academics on the subject, but simply to learn how to communicate better.

Just as Matthias didn't want to learn French but to talk to French women, with this book I don't want you to just learn postures, meanings of gestures and movements that you will surely forget easily; my goal is for you to completely change the way you communicate.

For my part, I promise to make it fun. Just follow me step by step, without rushing and realizing the success you'll achieve.

1

THE LINE THAT PASSES THROUGH YOUR BACK

To see clearly, just change the direction of your gaze.
- Antoine de Saint-Exupery

One of the benefits that technology has given us is the possibility of keeping in touch at all times; whether through social networks, instant messaging, e-mail or a simple phone call, we can say that we are permanently linked. This situation has more than a few detractors, who claim that dehumanization has begun with our growing dependence on mobile phones.

The zombie apocalypse started a long time ago as we all walk around like souls in pain with our faces stuck in a screen.

The real drawback of this situation is the posture we assume when interacting in this way. Almost invariably, we keep our head down, not taking our eyes off the half-composed text message, while both hands are held firmly gripping the phone against our solar plexus.

What are we conveying with this posture? An impassable force field, in which we do not allow anyone or anything to enter. And by "nothing" I mean attitudes, opinions, ideas, feelings. In short, any approach that requires any response on our part, both rational and emotional.

We think we're just fine like that; even when we let go of the communications toy, our head tends to stay tilted forward (and downwards), in a permanent gesture of not bothering. We live fast, and that posture shows it; we want to respond immediately to that instant message, while we finish composing the email to send it fleetingly before checking the status updates of our 300 friends.

Do you really think it's healthy to walk around all day with your head in a submissive position, staring at your phone? It's time to do something about it!

This is where our adventure begins: accepting that we live in a fast-paced age of frantic fingers on tiny keyboards, rushing and constant chores. But even as we become aware of our minute-to-minute rush, there is no excuse for neglecting the most important part of our image: posture. Straightening up, walking with our heads held high, looking around us, starting to "see" again what is happening in our immediate vicinity.

That's our first big step.

How long has it been since you enjoyed looking at the sky, admiring the treetops, the height of the buildings, or simply the eyes of others as you walk?

Presenting yourself slumped and with a crooked neck, not only makes you look insecure and weak.... it will also have a chemical effect on your mood. So from now on, from this very moment on.... You must consciously assume a correct posture at all times!

Regarding this last point, my first suggestion is that this is a habit that you must cultivate.

Assuming correct posture is pretty much what made us humans in the first place. Millions of years ago, we were primates who walked on all fours, exactly as gorillas do today. There was no problem if we moved short distances... And this position was very safe to protect our organs, which were partially exposed under the ribs.

But one day the fruit from the trees became scarce, and we all know that hunger is a great motivator. We had to cover greater and greater distances to get sustenance, and then those four legs became impractical. By standing upright, we invested less energy to move from one place to another, and the harsh sun of the plains no longer fell on our backs but only on our heads.

This modification of our posture brought us great benefits, especially to our hands, which, freed from locomotor work, became more and more refined and flexible. Suddenly, the silhouette of homo erectus emerged on the steppe, that *naked ape* of which Desmond Morris speaks, who would awaken one day to become the most intelligent animal of all.

How can we determine a correct standing posture? There are two ways, one perhaps more practical than the other: Standing with your back against a wall, stick your heels, buttocks and upper back against it. Ready? Now, a simple check: While still touching the wall at those three points, make sure that the arch formed by your lower back barely leaves room to put your outstretched hand. A little tricky, but if you've done it right and you feel comfortable, then that's the correct posture. Be sure to keep your chin aligned with the horizon.

Correct posture affects not only the way you look at the world, but also the flow of your energy. Your body will be better balanced and your back and abdominal muscles don't have to work as hard.

A second way to check your posture that you can apply in public is the axes rule. Simply imagine three axes, two horizontal and one vertical; the latter runs in a straight line from the top of your head, through your neck and down through your heart to your genitals. Ready? The two horizontal ones go through your shoulders and hips. Then simply imagine that the two horizontal axes are aligned at right angles to the vertical axis. That's it. You'll straighten yourself naturally, consciously, and in a concealed manner.

It is possible that your body rebels a little to this new posture. And I say "new", because you only have to look around: The lowered head, sunk into the chest, has practically become the norm.

Walking upright will also make others notice "something" in your presence; a sense of security, dominance and confidence that you will take advantage of later on.

Correct posture benefits your breathing, your digestion,

your circulation, the oxygenation of your brain... Are you going to throw away millions of years of evolution? It's in our nature: if we decided to get up one day and walk upright, we should continue to do so.

Don't forget to keep your chin aligned with the horizon. Make sure it points forward, not downward (looking at the phone) or upward (as in a haughty gesture). In any case, we will deal with it later.

Your challenge today:

Be sure to keep your eyes level with the horizon, where you can clearly see the eyes of others; where you can "see far away", and your sight is lost in the distance. As an additional ingredient, make sure your eyes never look at the floor (just don't trip over something...!).

Even if you have to communicate through your mobile phone, keep an eye on what's going on around you. Observe all the everyday things you have missed by having your face "buried" in your feet, in your thoughts or in your phone. Trees, clouds and buildings will greet you as if you're seeing them for the first time. And most importantly, you will start to see people's faces.... And your body will naturally straighten up.

Skills you will acquire with this exercise:

You will begin to develop your most important skill on this journey: observation. If until now you were used to "watch" the world without much interest, it is time to use your eyes proactively. You cannot interpret any gesture if you do not first learn to consciously detail everyday things.

Reclaim that sense of "discovery" that you enjoyed as a baby when you marveled at the world around you.

2

THE MOST IMPORTANT THING IN YOUR MOUTH

Laughter is the triumph of our beautiful gestures of creation over those of destruction.

- Peter Berger

One theme that both scientists and spiritual guides usually agree on is that the simple act of smiling can transform both you and the world around you. Both research and common sense have shown us that this expression is contagious. It can make us look more attractive, it lifts our spirits as well as those around us, and it can possibly make us live a little longer. So, before you read on, maybe it would be a good idea to smile for a few seconds - you'll thank me later!

When you smile, you secrete neuropeptides; these are small molecules that allow your neurons to communicate and help you release stress. These molecules facilitate the exchange of information between your brain and the rest of your body when you are happy, sad, angry, excited. Likewise, smiling recharges you with dopamine, endorphins, and serotonin, the happiness hormones. This not only relaxes your body, but also relaxes your heartbeat and blood pressure.

Your attractiveness increases when you smile; others treat you better because you project an image of confidence and sincerity. A study published in *Neuropsychology* reported that just by seeing a smiling face, you activate the occipitofrontal cortex of your brain, the area that processes rewards. This suggests that when you see a person smiling at you, you feel rewarded.

That also explains the results obtained by the Facial Research Laboratory at the University of Aberdeen, Scotland. Participants were asked to rate smiles and attractiveness, and found that both men and women chose more images that smiled and made eye contact than those that did not.

Smiling also has a contagious effect; the part of your brain that is responsible when you smile or imitate another's smile resides in the cingulate cortex, an area of automatic unconscious responses. In a study conducted in Sweden, subjects were shown pictures of different emotions such as Joy, Anger, Fear and Surprise. When presented with a smile, the researchers asked the subject to scrunch up their face; to their surprise, the first reaction was to imitate the smile in front of them. It took a conscious effort to make the requested grimace.

So if you smile at someone, they can't help but smile back. If they don't, it's because they are making a conscious effort to avoid it.

Even more impressive is knowing that every time you

smile at a person, their brain compels them to return the favor; you create a symbiotic response that allows you both to secrete beneficial chemicals in your brains, activate your reward centers, make you both more attractive and increase your chances of living a longer life.

In this image, you can see four smiles; between A and B, can you determine which one is true? [Answer: It is A]. you can see the crow's feet in the eyes as opposed to the less expressive B. In the case of C, we see the crow's feet but also an asymmetrical mouth, which is related to contempt. Finally, Nicholas Cage's smile in D can be misleading: it is a diplomatic smile, as there is no contraction of the eyes or cheeks, plus the corners of the lips point **downward.**

I have always thought that the Japanese are very thrifty in their expressiveness, as well as with their architecture and decoration; nothing seems to be superfluous. How about comparing a western smiling emote with one from the Land of the Rising Sun?

:-)   (^_^)

Indeed, while in one we see neutral eyes and a smiling mouth, it is enough for the Japanese version to have both eyes squinted. And that is the heart of this expression... the "crow's feet" are necessary, inevitable, to show joy!

Our parents always told us that everything in excess is bad, and in the case of smiling, there is no exception. Have you ever come across one of those people who smiles the same way to everyone? It seems that their feelings are indecipherable... they can't be happy all the time!

Personally, I have a bad feeling about this kind of people. I always trust more in a face occasionally "tied" by bitterness (which I know will not be false) than in those who boast perpetually cheerful teeth. Don't hide your smile, but don't spread it left and right either. Being measured will make you look authentic, approachable and trustworthy.

¿Muestra los dientes inferiores?
No es una sonrisa auténtica.

Don't forget the speed of your smile!

Scientist have determined that smiles that take more than half a second to form are the ones that generate the most trust and attraction.

Who can be attracted to a nervous smile that is triggered by virtually any stimulus? Take it easy and smile slowly!

Your challenge today:

Practice your 'real' smile in front of the mirror. How could you define what it feels like to see yourself smile? Could it be improved? Practice various intensities, from a mildly smiling face to a fully open smile.

Be aware of your smile; it is your best business card.

Skills you will acquire with this exercise:

You will learn to smile even in the moments when you don't feel particularly good. You will see that this will be very useful to you, and you will realize that even though people smile, there are often small details that do not fit with a happy attitude.

3

YOUR INTUITION

The only truly valuable thing is intuition.
 - Albert Einstein

What's the first thing that comes to mind when someone brings up the subject of body language? Some instantly say *"If you cross your arms you are closed"* (I don't know exactly what they mean by "closed"), or *"If you touch your nose, you are lying"*, *"If you drag your feet you are moping"*, *"If someone (twists - twitches - moves - turns up - turns) their (mouth - hand - eyes - chest) then they are (sad - happy - pensive)"*

You get the idea.

Most books on nonverbal communication only feed this tendency, satisfying the left hemisphere of your brain: it loves to interpret things literally because A means A, and it is not possible that it means B or C. But this approach is too simple, because something as complex as kinesics cannot be categorized as we do with words.

How could you interpret body language if you don't have a "chart" to tell you the meaning of each gesture?

Before running you must learn to walk. And even if you had a meaning for each gesture, it would be impossible to decipher on the fly, because... how many gestures, tics and movements of each part of the body do you notice in a conversation? Tens or even hundreds! A titanic and impossible task, to decipher them on the fly...!

Visualize this simple scene:

You are talking to your boss about a sensitive subject about which you want to "get" relevant information out of him; paying attention to the movement of his eyes, the tone of his voice, the gestures of his hands, his posture, the times he touches his hair, plays with a fountain pen, rubs his hands against his pants, crosses his arms, legs, snorts....

Suddenly you realize that you haven't paid attention to his words!

Even if you take into account only the basics of nonverbal language, the complete analysis of a static pose (without taking facial expressions into account) can be a frustrating task for the uneducated eye.

Before you start getting desperate trying to determine things like head tilt, how tightly your arms are crossed, palm orientation, and eventual finger tension, answer one simple question:

What feeling does this image inspire in you? (Look at it for about 30 seconds, then read on).

Situations like this present themselves to us on a daily basis. We want to interpret nonverbal language, but we get distracted by details before we relax and try to access our intuition; after doing so, you can unravel each gesture as you wish.

For example, I don't know what the seated man inspired in you, but he inspired some wariness in me. I'm going to jump ahead to some characteristics to explain: both the gaze and the foot forward toward us indicate attention; but when someone is really paying attention, they tend to tilt their head a little to one side, so, since his head is straight up, he's actually **alert.**

On the other hand, the legs are tightly crossed and propped up with fingers interlocked; it's like being sheltered inside a fortress. If you want to persuade someone to have this posture, you must first get them out of it.

This is when the right hemisphere comes into play. That is the key to deciphering that tangle of gestures, as it has always been there to do so (even if you don't pay much attention to it). The detail is that his approach is much more holistic; it determines the overall meaning of a person's whole "body phrase" and then looks for little clues to confirm its hypothesis.

Don't you notice that this is how we read? You don't stop to think about the meaning of each word individually, but absorb each sentence as a whole, and in some cases you can understand a paragraph just by glancing at it.

Apply this reading technique to body language. Forget once and for all that you are going to learn a "sign book", and focus on what you feel when someone speaks or walks.

You must be careful: Your left hemisphere, so rational, so accustomed to the logic of 2+2=4, will do everything possible to interfere. Why bother trusting in something as "ethereal" as intuition, if we can be guided only by words?

This seduction of logic will assail you frequently, and even more so now as you begin to study the secrets of nonverbal communication.

Like all mental faculties, intuition is a muscle. If you dedicate yourself to flexing it every day by calming your logical reasoning and letting yourself be guided by what you perceive in an impartial and direct way, it will become easier and easier.

This skill has always been with you since you were born, you just forgot how to use it: to interpret the silent signals of gestures and facial expressions.

You may have heard the theories of proud grandmothers who claimed that their newborn grandchildren had an uncanny sensitivity to detect when someone who is 'negatively charged' (or in other words, had a bad day), came over to play with them. Immediately the baby would become apprehensive and even tearful.

The reality is that we all come into the world with an interpretation "kit" for nonverbal communication, which is indispensable for our survival in the first months of life when we do not even pronounce a single word.

Thanks to that ability we can detect even the slightest frown that our dad got from his job, or the caring movements of our mother's arms. Not only that: at that age we are experts at recognizing voices... and although we don't know what they say, we know what they *want* to say.

We grow up and become more and more dependent on words; what better than simply say we're hungry when we want to eat? It's much more efficient than the bunch of signs we make (of which crying seems to be the most effective).

When you grow up, you forget your kinesthetic abilities; but they are still there, waiting for you to use them again. It is as if as soon as you were born, you were put in a wheelchair, even though your legs worked fine. Years go by, and suddenly one day someone says to you:

"Hey, get up, you don't need the chair...you were born with a pair of legs you can walk on."

At first incredulous, you would put such a statement to the test... but after years of not using them, it will not be easy for you to walk right away. It is only after a good effort that you will be able to regain control of them.

Do you want to regain your ability to interpret non-verbal language?

You must start with the key word:

Serenity.

A boiling mind, an altered temperament, an uneasy personality will make the process of observation and analysis of gestures more difficult.

Start by relaxing your frown, that wrinkle you have on your forehead every time you want to make a "deep analysis" of things. It may take you a while.

Observe with serenity and try not to be disturbed by anything.

A Very Important Note: How to differentiate your intuition... from your prejudices?

At times, you may think you are tapping into your intuition... when in fact you are filtering reality through your own biases.

How can you be sure that this is not the case? It is important that you know how to apply this little tip in real time...

Start by isolating a single gesture. For example, if they cross their arms if you start talking.

Now, imagine two people: someone you like very much and someone you dislike very much, making exactly the same gesture in the same situation.

If in all cases you perceive the same thing, it is intuition. If you feel that the gesture changes according to the affinity with the person, it's a prejudice.

Your challenge today:

Start by observing people carefully and try to isolate yourself from what they say, concentrating on their posture. Try to sum up what you feel when you see them in one word: Joy. Concern. Disappointed. Excited. Insecure. Anxious.

Remember that this faculty is programmed in your non-rational side; just make a conscious effort to let it flow.

Try doing it in a public place such as a coffee shop or restaurant where you can see other people chatting. Be discreet, of course!

Skills you will acquire with this exercise:

You will begin to develop your intuition for nonverbal language, which is essential to be able to interpret these silent signals quickly.

Watch like when you were a baby. Don't reason, just feel it.

4

BREATHING

There is a common circulation, a common breath; we are all connected.

- Hippocrates

The myths surrounding nonverbal communication have not ceased to appear in our daily entertainment sessions, particularly on the small screen. Early and tentatively in series like CSI, the abilities of some detectives to "read" criminals as if they were discount coupons became increasingly common in the standard curriculum of fictional officers.

Then came "Lie to Me", in which Cal Lightman (played by Tim Roth) plays the virtual double of none other than Paul Ekman, an American scientist who pioneered the study of facial micro-expressions and emotions on the face.

Ekman is, in fact, technical advisor for that series... or

should be was, because after three seasons it was cancelled. Apparently the numbers did not support the contract renewal, but considering that body language has so many fans, how is it possible that a series that revolves around this topic, succumbed so quickly?

Personally, the problem I saw with the plot was the all-powerful tools they applied: they often provided too quick solutions to the riddles. At the other end of the spectrum, Dr. Lightman was an overly visceral and even aggressive character.

I consider that the series that best approaches body language reading is "The Mentalist", whose main character (Patrick Jane, played by Simon Baker) takes things much more calmly and focused. Paul Ekman himself has emphasized an unattractive reality of this medium: Analyzing human emotions is not a job that can be done under pressure. If you put Lightman and Jane in a ring with these rules of the game, the latter would come out on top.

Remember the calm and serenity you began to develop in the previous exercise? Real-life mentalists engage in tricks that completely baffle their audiences. From complex card divination games to detecting "by ethereal inspiration" a cardiovascular condition in one of the attendees at their presentations, these persuasion artists base their extraordinary powers on a single word:

Hypersensitivity.

Literally, they are sponges for everything that happens around them.

Marc Salem, a renowned mentalist, has a spectacular demonstration: he asks you, through a phone call, to think of a number from 1 to 100. Then you must count, starting from

I... and he is able to stop you at the exact number you thought of, without ever failing.

How does it do it?

Salem is not shy about explaining that it is not a trick, but simply learning to become aware of his own breathing. This allows him to relax, to become more sensitive and to be able to "read" that of others; he can then detect the moment when his interlocutor holds his breath a little longer than usual when mentioning the chosen number.

Breathing is one of the easiest body processes to consciously modify. Think, for example, that you want to change your heart rate; unless you experience a sudden emotion, you will not be able to do it just by thinking about it or wanting to do it. Imagine now that you wanted to digest food faster than normal. Impossible!

Instead, take a moment to breathe deeply, right now.

A single inspiration.

Super easy, right? how would you like to do it while being questioned by the police? Well, it changes things up a bit...! It turns out that your breathing is also affected by your emotions; to the extent that you feel anxious or threatened, you feel short of breath and need to take in air more frequently and more intensely.

It is an inescapable reality.

How about if instead of being a "random breather", you dedicate yourself to controlling this process? Since it is automatic, you have not bothered to develop or perfect it. From now on you can benefit from a simple exercise that you can do anywhere, but you should assign it to a particular event: for example, the time it takes for the traffic light to change to green.

How long will it take? Ten seconds? Twenty? It doesn't matter.

In those brief moments, breathe as follows: breathe in as deeply as possible, very slowly and quietly (the quieter you do it, the better), until you feel your belly expand completely. Hold your breath for a second or two and then exhale (again, without making a sound). Four or five times is enough. Repeat at least three times a day.

Isn't it not complicated at all?

It may seem strange for a kinesics guide to include such exercises, but if you remember the importance of relaxing, being alert and being able to identify the subtlest reactions in others (and even keep your composure if you discover that they are openly lying to you), you will understand that it is necessary to develop a good breathing habit.

The next step: Box breathing

Box breathing' is a tip that will help you develop your focus and attention in the moment; it not only helps you calm down but also helps you focus on the task at hand.

Look at the following diagram...

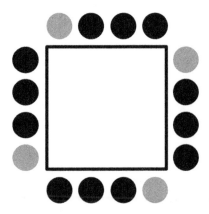

It is called 'box breathing', because you imagine a box with four circles on each side. Each circle equals either one second, or one beat of your heart.

First, you breathe in for four seconds or beats; then you hold your breath for four more, expel it for another cycle of four and finally, leave your lungs empty for the remaining four.

That is all.

Try it right now. How does it feel?

An important detail...

Once you become aware of your own breathing, it is crucial that you try to observe the breathing of others. This is accomplished in two ways: by watching the rhythm of their chest and shoulders, or by listening when they speak and take a breath between each sentence.

Your challenge today:

Get into the habit of doing this exercise every day. Then, think about your breathing when you are having a conversation. How does it feel? Does it feel choppy, or does it work normally?

Skills you will acquire with this exercise:

Self-control. In the art of persuasion, 50% of success is knowing your interlocutor... and the other 50% is knowing yourself. How do you expect to get to 100% if you have no control over your own non-verbal reactions? And in order to control them, you first have to become fully aware of them!

In your breath is your strength and power.

5

HOW TO PAY ATTENTION

The best gift we can give someone is our undivided attention.
- Richard Moss

These days, concentration is definitely a luxury. From the moment we wake up in the morning until we fall asleep at night, we are subjected to an unprecedented barrage of messages and stimuli through the most diverse channels.

That's why until a few days ago, we were walking around with our faces in our phones...!

Our attention span, which some studies used to set at just over fifteen minutes, has decreased to a few seconds: practically the length of a movie trailer. Even when we seem to be listening to our boss as he tells us something relevant to the future of the company (and our position!), we are thinking about a thousand things simultaneously:

Did I lock the car door properly? Did I send that memo last week? Isn't it Aunt Peppa's birthday these days...?

In the figure, a girl has exactly the same expression, only in one of the instances her head is tilted very slightly, which happens when we pay real attention to what we are listening to and at the same time, we are storing it in our memory.

Chances are you haven't finished reading this page and already have some paranoia related to the subject; but before you put the book aside to verify that you programmed the TV to record *Game of Thrones*, remember that keeping your full attention when they talk to you is a habit that will be very useful not only in learning body language, but for your life. How many misunderstandings and arguments could you save yourself daily just by listening carefully to what they say to you?

It doesn't cost you anything to try: concentrate, really concentrate on the person who is talking to you.

Eye contact is most important in this case, as it is a direct bridge to a full understanding of the meaning of the words. When you are in this state of alertness, your head will "drop" slightly to one side. Likewise, your frown (which you have already learned to relax) will not be furrowed by vertical lines that can be interpreted as judgments or doubts.

Such mindfulness will produce a sense of well-being in others, and you will earn a reputation as a great conversationalist.

Simply by listening carefully!

Your challenge today:

Next time you have a conversation, give it your undivided attention. If you start to wander off thinking about the vegetables you have to buy at the market, you'll notice your neck getting tense and you'll stop nodding your head.

Pay attention to everything they tell you, and form a vivid mental image of every detail you catch; that way you will remember them more easily the next time you talk to that person.

Demonstrating that you remember what you are told is an excellent way to be liked and build trust.

Skills you will acquire with this exercise:

Not only will you learn to focus on what others are expressing to you, you will also take the first step in detecting when they are not paying attention to you. It's a good practice that will pay off down the road, you'll see!

Now, stop for a moment... and really listen. They will thank you.

6

THE POWER OF A SQUEEZE

With a clenched fist you cannot exchange a handshake.
- Indira Gandhi

Of all the gestures in the world, the classic handshake is undoubtedly the most universal of all. Socially accepted in the vast majority of circumstances, how can we go wrong when we shake hands?

Unfortunately, the reality is different: How defective are the handshakes we receive on a daily basis! The hand may be sweaty and cold, it may be parched or visibly dirty (yes, I'm talking about that "mustache" that some people's fingernails sport), or it may be limp (or ready to crush our bones). There are a hundred different ways to spoil this approach.

Is there a formula for the perfect handshake? Yes, there

is... but it does us no good if we don't translate it into our daily experience.

One of the most important ingredients of this greeting has nothing to do with hands: eye contact. Maintaining it before, during and after the handshake is essential. No matter who you're shaking hands with or the circumstances... you should always do it. But, how are you going to "hit" your hand against the other person's, if you are looking them straight in the eye...?

You don't have to worry about "getting it right" with your handshake if you extend your hand first.

"Who...? Me...? Reach out first...? No way!"

You may not be shy enough to tell me this, but I'm sure you're a little worried about being left holding your hand out, and so you may be waiting for the other person to take the initiative.

But this initiative gives the other person the image of proactivity and decisiveness, and leaves you with the silver medal of simply answering the greeting.

Why don't you extend your hand first, thus projecting a decisive and confident personality? And you don't need to break eye contact!

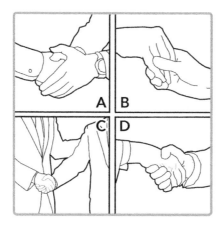

In the images, we see four different handshakes: In A the hands of both maintain a neutral angle, which is correct; however, one of them 'hugs' the handshake with another hand, wanting to project warmth... but not a good idea. It is much better to project that quality through full eye contact and a smile.

In B it is a common mistake; either both hands are not at the right angle, or they do not make full contact as they should, or worse: the handshake is bland on the part of one or both. In all cases, the impression left by the person is one of disinterest.

In C, it's a classic political handshake: One of them (the one who wants to project power), draws the handshake toward himself to give the impression that it was the other who had to approach (one approaches to greet the person of higher rank, like wanting to greet a king). The other hand on the arm projects cordiality; it is a balance of two contrasting terms in one gesture, and well worth practicing.

Finally, in D we see that one of the two has forced the handshake to keep the palm down, which is known as the dominant handshake; it is a power play in the handshake where obviously both people cannot do it at the same time. That's why it's so important to take the initiative and reach out one's hand first.

You can always offer a 'neutral grip', as in this image. Keep your fingers relaxed and with little or no palm tilt relative to the floor.

Your challenge today:

Learn to shake hands first, without breaking eye contact. If your hands are sweaty, keep a handkerchief in your pants pocket, coat pocket or purse to dry them quickly in anticipation of an introduction or greeting. Make sure your nails are well trimmed and clean, and a moisturizer is a must.

Well-groomed hands are an excellent standard of hygiene and professionalism.

Skills you will acquire with this exercise:

You will take the first steps to develop self-confidence and build the foundations of your ability to persuade and convince.

Time to shake hands. Don't forget... you first.

7

YOUR PERIPHERAL VISION

Look not back in anger, nor forward in fear, but round about with attention.

- James Thurker

When learning to interpret body language, one of the most important skills to develop is your observation skills.

Your eyes are a very curious tool; you have a very wide field of vision (180 degrees from side to side and 100 degrees vertically), and you generally use only a small fraction of it to the fullest. There is a certain difference between women and men, as the male brain processes panoramic information with certain reservations compared to the female brain. Hence, a woman is less likely to be hit by a car (precisely because of this condition).

Watching people can make them uncomfortable, unless

you do it indirectly. How do you think you could get a sense of what's going on in a whole group at once? That's where your panoramic vision comes into play, allowing you to appreciate postures, gestures and even facial expressions out of the corner of your eye.

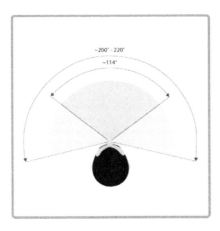

Just as you read without having to stop at every letter or word, you can "scan" your surroundings without having to stare at people.

Your challenge today:

Develop your peripheral vision with this exercise: when watching a series, movie or video, don't look directly at the screen. Instead, step back a little and look away from the screen, at an angle of at least 45 degrees. To make the exercise easier, fix your gaze on an object.

Skills you will develop with this exercise:

At first you may find it a little difficult, but you will see that with just fifteen minutes a day it will be easier to notice what is going on around you.

Let's go, to look out of the corner of your eye... So that you don't get caught analyzing others!

8

ARE YOU PASSIONATE WITH YOUR GESTURES?

Passion is a chronic emotion.

- Théodule Armand-Ribot

Am I too gestual? I move my hands a lot when I talk... Is that good or bad? I feel that people notice me nervous! Should I control my gestures?

These are some of the most frequently asked questions when we talk about kinesics. Becoming aware of one's own gestures generates great interest in anyone, and many think that by controlling them they are "restricting their personality", when in fact, this is not the case.

Think of two scenarios: in the first, you present a project to the managers of the company where you work, wanting to impress them so that it is approved (and perhaps qualify for a promotion).

In the second, it's the weekend, and you're having a Sunday barbecue with your friends and a few beers.

Will the vocabulary and attitude you use in each case be the same?

I don't think so.

In this way, we are refuting the hypothesis that claims that controlling or modeling your body language is limiting your personality. Not at all!

Are you not being yourself when you want to impress your bosses? Or are you doing it with your friends? Nothing of the sort; you're simply adapting to situations... and in life we come across many and opposite to each other.

Just as you control your vocabulary and the way you express yourself, why not also control your body language?

The main problem for all of us is that under certain circumstances, our gestures seem to stop completely, while in others they reach almost frantic movements.

When you are nervous or uncomfortable you put one hand on top of the other, put them in your pockets, place them behind your back or even hide them under your crossed arms; and when you get too excited when you speak, you raise your voice to make yourself heard above others, make very loud and broad gestures and seek to make your opinion heard. In both cases, you face an imbalance.

These images will explain a bit about why it doesn't matter so much how *many* gestures you make, but *how you make them and how they support your message:*

In the image, a woman is giving a public speech; note the height at which she has her hands. This area (area A) is where most of your gestures should take place, no matter how much you do. Area B, at the height of the face, should be limited only to emphasis and very important points you want to highlight. The reason? We transmit so much through the face, and bringing your hands close to it can distract rather than reinforce the message.

Regarding width, you can make all the gestures you want as long as they remain slightly wider than shoulder width.

You can also 'go outside' these limits, but only when your speech or your message requires it; if you need to get your interlocutor or your audience excited, it will be necessary.

The last detail to consider is the tension in your hands. Keep them relaxed whenever you can; tension, such as clawing them in the image, even talking with clenched fists, should be reserved for very strong emphasis. Remember that the protagonist is **your message,** not you.

You must start paving the road of persuasion. A persuasive person is neither faint-hearted nor exalted; he or she just manages to convince us with a solution that we think is great.

Want to convince others of your point of view? Moderate speed gestures are the key.

Your challenge today:

Learn to recognize the speed and amplitude of your own gestures; it is the first step to control it. Everyone's "balance point" is different, and some of us are more expressive than others; it all depends on the situation and your mood.

You must identify two phases: when you feel nervous and your gestures slow down, and when you are excited and look like a mime playing ping pong. Only then will you discover your middle ground, your speed of persuasion.

Skills you will acquire with this exercise:

Be aware of your nonverbal expression style. Although at first it may seem awkward and even unpleasant, it is essential for making future adjustments.

You have your work cut out for you today, so identify the intensity of your gestures!

9

TIME TO EXPAND YOUR SPACE

A man's personality determines in advance the measure of
his possible fortune.
- Arthur Schopenauer

Have you ever wondered what our fascination with giant screens is? Why watching a movie in an extra-large format is better than a small one?

Perhaps it has something to do with immersion; as a stimulus encompasses more of your visual field, it will be more impactful and more easily remembered.

Something similar happens with the peacock's feathers: it uses them to "cover more space" in the female's field of vision, not only using their attractiveness but also their extension and movement.

Alpha and Beta positions

This has to do with the term 'Alpha and Beta Postures', which refer to hierarchy in the animal world, and we do not escape that classification.

Alpha postures refer to the dominant members of the group, and betas to the submissive or those who 'follow' the leaders.

For a better understanding, take a look at this image:

I already mentioned it on day 3: in the first instants you should let your intuition guide you. Obviously I can't know what feeling you get from each of these positions, but I can ask you the question: which ones would you consider dominant, and which ones submissive?

The answer: Alpha postures are 1 and 4; Beta postures are 2 and 3. As for their characteristics, you will notice that in an Alpha posture a high chin and a straight posture are a must; slightly expanding the elbows is also a common factor.

On the contrary, Beta postures 'tuck in' and slouch slightly, and what can you say about their feet? Exactly: they move closer together.

Does this mean that you always have to assume an Alpha posture? Well, it is ideal if you are going to speak in public, if you have to convince a group or if in general, you have to be persuasive or exercise leadership; but sometimes, a beta posture can be very useful. The example may sound creepy, but in case of a kidnapping it is probably a good idea to assume a beta posture in front of your captors, while waiting for an opportunity to escape.

We have another example, in comics: imagine you're reading one of Superman's and when you get to the end, you see in the last frame the triumphant Man of Steel, in his typical pose: standing with his chest out and his hands resting on his hips. Remember what happens with his elbows? He looks "heroic", and spans *more space than usual.*

Another image to illustrate this point...

Can you perceive the difference between these two attitudes?

Don't think I'm going to ask you to assume this position all day long either (you'd look a little weird!), and there's a reason both comic writers and the peacock save these bodily manifestations for special moments: to emphasize one's personality, attitude, character.

Can you tell the difference in attitude, just by moving your
feet a little apart?

A hormonal effect on your personality

Part of the findings of Amy Cuddy, a social psychologist at
Harvard University, revolve around the effect this posture has
on our attitude: the mere fact of assuming this position before
a stressful situation (such as a business presentation, for
example), chemically helps you to be better prepared to
face it.

That's what Alpha and Beta poses are all about; Superman's pose is an Alpha one, demonstrating power and leadership. It is assumed by those who lead, who take charge, who
take responsibility.

Alpha postures are characterized by having the feet firmly
planted on the floor, chest out, shoulders relaxed and trying
to cover as much space as possible with the body.

The opposite pole are the Beta poses that refer to the
followers, those who are dependent, those who are submissive in one way or another. They are characterized by keeping

the limbs close to the body, the chin low and keeping eye contact to a minimum.

Your challenge today:

You're used to crossing your arms when you want to be emphatic and express that you don't plan to change your mind; but much better than that is to assume, in a relaxed manner, a posture where one or both elbows stick out a little.

Another alternative is to gesture with the hands *while keeping the elbows away from the body.*

Skills you will acquire with this exercise:

A natural posture doesn't have to be submissive. Get used to staying in 'Alpha" most of the time (but don't forget the goodness of a Beta posture). As far as intensity goes, remember that if both hands are on your hips and both elbows are fully out, you can look threatening.

Don't forget to practice (the mirror is good for something!).

Oh, and I almost forgot one last detail: if you put your hands in your pants pockets, you will break the effect completely.

Get noticed. Don't go unnoticed.

10

ILLUSTRATORS, OR MANIPULATORS?

You have in your hands the color of your day: routine or burst.

- Mario Benedetti

It's amazing how many different ways you move your hands while conversing. Their variety and frequency depend on your gestural "personality": some people gesture a lot with their fingers and palms, others are sparing in their manual expression.

On this day what you are really interested in is identifying the three main types of hand movements you employ in those daily interactions:

Illustrating gestures

These are the ones that complement the conversation, and convey ideas naturally with a continuous flow. For example, if you say someone used to be very fat, you might place your arms as if hugging an imaginary barrel... or while describing a very tall person you raise one hand and look up.

But the main defining characteristic of an illustrator is that you employ it for a **purpose**. Although an illustrative gesture by itself has no meaning, it supports speech either passively or actively. Some examples:

In these four images we can study different approaches to the use of illustrators; the popular 'Hands in bell tower', (A) is a **passive** illustrative gesture which projects confidence and decisiveness; it is widely used by leaders in various fields. It is a perfect example of a gesture that *does not have a direct meaning* but connotes a quality that we want to project.

In (B) we see an **active** illustrative gesture which consists of supporting a numbering or list that we are saying out loud by making the gesture of counting with our fingers. It is a perfect example of how illustrative gestures complement our words and allow us to communicate both verbally and bodily in unison to be more convincing.

The speaker in (C) uses the open hands **actively** not to

support his speech, but to make his image broader (As what I exposed in the previous lesson), and to involve his audience by directing the illustrators towards them. 'Drawing attention' we could claim to be his intention, or emphasizing a general idea.

In (D), the hand gesture itself doesn't say much, unless you take into account the openness of the fingers; *any* illustrator changes nuance depending on this factor, with fingers spread apart and relaxed being an image of confidence and tranquility, while fingers together and firm are decisiveness and firmness.

Continuing with examples of illustrators, in the previous figure both A and B are variations of the clenched fist, which in the former is more relaxed (thus serving to project authority and firmness without being imposing), while in B the fist clenches a little more, being a more powerful gesture to give even more firmness to one's arguments.

The opposite pole would be the illustrator in C, who seeks to appease tempers by slightly showing both palms (a practically universal gesture of non-aggression), and the hands slightly together, almost protecting the chest. Note the contrast with D, in which the hands are in exactly the same position as in C, but the combination of fist and extended index finger gives them an aggressive and emphatic connotation.

It is very difficult to fake illustrative gestures, and it is very common to see a political speech where the speaker has illustrators "out of time", because he has not been sufficiently prepared to transmit this naturalness.

By the way: the illustrators used in public speaking are called "Baton gestures".

Attention to the illustrators in which the palm is shown repeatedly: the person may be looking for some kind of justification for his actions...

...he may even be lying and is looking for us to believe him.

Manipulative gestures

Manipulators are absolutely unnecessary, superfluous and disruptive gestures; instead of supporting the discourse, they interrupt it and run over it. They are the "crutches" of the conversation, such as scratching the nose, scratching the ears, stretching the cuffs of the shirt, shaking an imaginary lint out of the coat, running the hand through the hair....

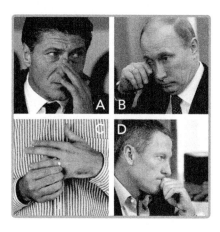

They will usually be accompanied by words like "Uhm...", "Estee...", "Eeeh...", as they are an indication of two things: 1) You are not sure of what you are saying (either because of nerves or because you have not mastered the subject), and 2) The situation implies a strong emotional attachment to you.

(You are unlikely to manifest manipulators if you are asked for an address you know well).

The emblems

Emblems are gestures that have a pre-agreed meaning for a particular culture, such as the "OK" sign and the thumbs-up. I do not recommend using them much, as their meaning often varies radically from one culture to another.

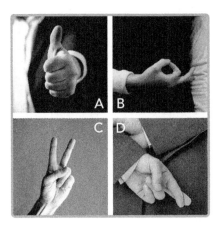

These are emblems that exhibit a specific meaning that may not necessarily transfer across cultures. For example, (A) generally means "Good job", although in some European countries it is an obscene gesture; (B) means "Money" in Japan, regardless of the meaning it may have in some Latin American countries. Likewise, C and D could mean to us "Victory" and "Luck" respectively, but you should use them with caution when traveling.

To classify the emblems and their meaning in each country would take a whole book!

Your challenge today:

Identify, throughout this day, whether the gestures you use are illustrative, manipulative or emblematic. When do you use them? You will find that illustrators come naturally when you are convinced of what you are talking about; manipulators will come out of nervousness (of whatever intensity).

As for emblems, just try not to abuse them.

Skills you will acquire with this exercise:

You will learn to identify what situations make you nervous and why... and you will begin to control your manipulators.

(Which we will put to the test... very soon!)*)

The more illustrators you use, the more confident you look.

11

THE RELEVANCE OF THE CONTEXT

The true meaning is found by saying the same things, but with other words.
- Charles Chaplin

Do you remember lesson 7, where you learned to observe your environment in a general way? I hope you have practiced it several times, because today you are going to take a step forward.

You will discover that body language, like words, has its own semantics.

There is no better way to illustrate this than using the example of the word "Bark". What mental image do you form when you read it? Can you imagine a dog barking? Or perhaps the outer sheath of a tree?

Or you remember it's slang for crazy!

Context has a direct influence on the meaning of words, and in body language it is exactly the same: It is not a matter of relying solely on facial expressions, or on hands, or even on posture; you have to follow a logical order that allows you to organize the information you receive, and for this you will analyze, in order, seven factors: **situation, environment, proximity, posture, gestures, voice volume and facial expressions.**

The **situation** determines the direct reason for which the communication is established. For example, it is a police interrogation, or two people talking over coffee. In this case, you may wonder *why the interaction is taking place.*

The **environment** indicates the physical conditions of the communication. Is there a lot of noise from traffic or people? (this can condition proximity), Is the lighting sufficient or poor, is it hot or cold? Reviewing these factors before proceeding with the kinesthetic analysis is crucial.

Proximity or proxemics forces you to specify the distance between the two people, which is conditioned by the situation and the environment.

The **posture** will tell you how uncomfortable or relaxed the speaker is, if there is a predisposition (if they approach each other) or their excitement and interest.

The **hand gestures** will remind you of the previous lesson: Are you using illustrators, manipulators or emblems...?

Facial expressions, due to their special difficulty to pinpoint "in real time", will be discussed a little later.

Your challenge today:

It studies the first five factors (situation, environment,

proximity, posture and gestures) in a minimum of four different scenarios.

I recommend using pencil and paper.

Skills you will acquire with this exercise:

You will begin to prioritize the factors involved in nonverbal communication and interpret them "on the fly".

Never lose track of everything going on around you!

12

THE EFFECTS OF EYE CONTACT

Whoever does not understand a look, will not understand a long explanation either.

- Arabic Proverb

When we meet a threatening dog in the street, one of the first actions that comes to our mind is to try to alter it as little as possible. On the one hand, we should not smile (showing our teeth is a clear provocation in the animal kingdom), and on the other hand, it is better to turn our body to the other side and follow it with the corner of our eye.

This preprogramming (eye contact/threat) interferes with your daily relationships. Shyness and the desire to go unnoticed may lead you to avoid the gaze of others, on pain of "invading their space", threatening their privacy or even intruding on their thoughts.

In most cases, an exchange of glances between two strangers tends to break right away, due to this prejudice imposed by inadequate conditioning.

Did you know that your brain has a circuit board specialized in face recognition? That's why that cloud we see in the sky looks very similar to Aunt Pepa. And that one over there, Beethoven; and between the two, we see a frozen dragon yawning.

If you have never had problems establishing eye contact, this time do it consciously. And if you have always had trouble establishing that bridge between your eyes and those of your interlocutor, look for a point above the septum of the nose, where you can fix your gaze; you will see, with a little effort, that it is not so difficult.

Do you have a hard time maintaining eye contact? Look for the midpoint between the two eyes, and notice it.

Your challenge today:

Double the frequency with which you look at people in the eyes. If this is not a problem for you, then do it consciously; start to detail the movements of the pupils and create a "profile". Are they slow or erratic movements? Do they constantly turn their eyes away? Do the eyelids droop a little, or are they fully open? Try to ask yourself all these questions (without losing the thread of the conversation, of course).

Skills you will acquire with this exercise:

You will get used to holding your gaze; you should be able to do this without feeling any discomfort. When you achieve this, begin to detail the shape, movements and characteristics of the eyes. Your attention span will be enhanced, as you will learn to concentrate on faces... a condition that will be very useful to you in a short time.

13

SIT DOWN; WE NEED TO TALK

Some people start talking just before they think.

- Jean de la Bruyére

Can there be a more emotionally stressful time in a professional environment than a job interview? That uncertainty you have about the verdict? What could tip the balance in your favor?

You make sure you have a complete and orderly resume, you are punctual, you dress impeccably... and you let yourself be carried away by your nerves at the very moment when you should be calmer and in perfect control of the situation.

One of the factors that affect your attitude in these circumstances is sitting. Ergonomically, it is neither natural nor beneficial to your body, apart from restricting your nonverbal expression. You may try to calm yourself by shaking a leg, which results in even greater concern about controlling it.

Being aware of your own posture and that of your inter-locutor is essential, since most of the persuasion occurs when we are seated. Not only job interviews, but also meetings of all kinds are conducted in this position.

This is an example of a 'neutral' position, in which the back is kept straight and slightly tilted back, shoulders relaxed, hands in the lap and feet straight on the floor. In the case of wearing a skirt, the posture can be adapted, as in this example:

The variation in this case is the minimal inclination of the trunk, and the legs together or crossed at the ankles. So far, the projected message is the same: **Attention.**

The inclination of the trunk is a variable to be considered according to the **interest** shown by the person. For example.

We tilt our body towards what catches our attention, and in this case the man leans because he considers what he is listening to to be important. The opposite case is the following...

...in which a more comfortable position has been sought, leaning on the backrest.

When it comes to crossing the legs for comfort or to vary the posture, it is important that the sole of the shoe does not point towards the person with whom we are communicating, but points to the floor.

Nothing complicated... until you realize that in stressful situations you place your legs as straight as possible, with your feet firmly on the floor. Who can be comfortable like that? The best is to cross one leg over the other, but if you follow the second rule, you must be careful to turn subtly so as not to "aggress" with the sole of your shoe.

The expansion of lesson 9 also applies when we are seated. For example, on the one hand, we can try to cover the field of view like this:

And we can do the opposite:

Throughout an interview, it is common for you to demonstrate both illustrators and manipulators, and for your mouth muscles to be more tense than usual with a consequent loss of verbal fluency. It is common that in tense moments like this, you unwittingly assume such postures:

You will find that when you learn to sit in a relaxed and confident manner, you will be able to express yourself better and have a better command of the situation.

Your challenge today:

Learn to become aware of the way you feel. Are you

relaxed and comfortable, or the opposite? It will be difficult at first due to lack of practice and focus.

Skills you will acquire with this exercise:

You will be able to feel more confident in stressful situations and where you have to convince someone while sitting down. Remember that the way you control your legs is the first step to mastering the situation.

By the way, how are you sitting now?

14

THE TIME TO TALK

The second is the first of the losers.
- Ayrton Senna

Ask yourself a simple question: What are you communicating for?

The answer is not difficult to state, but it is a little difficult to explain.

You engage in communication when you ask for some kind of information: perhaps an address, a phone number or an email. All easily answered, because there is no emotional commitment. But what if you have to determine if someone is lying about a crime?

Do you think it will be just as easy?

In one case or another, we assume that the person who "breaks the ice" has the need for certain information... And the person who responds is providing -whether he/she wants it or not- the data sought. In other words, the respondent is in control of the conversation, as he/she is the one who *ultimately decides whether the conversation progresses or not.*

This dynamic is simple to understand, until you realize that in persuasion and seduction, the process is the other way around:

The icebreaker creates a factor of dependence on himself, to the point that he is able not only to originate the conversation, but also to determine the direction it will take.

At first you take into account very simple techniques such as asking "open" questions, to which you can not answer with a simple yes or no; but then you realize that it is not only about your interlocutor to express himself, but to talk about what you want.

How many times have you wanted to "get information" out of someone without them realizing it?

Beyond using hypnosis or some other unethical resource, one of the easiest ways is to simply *ask first.*

But in this process you have not considered a crucial factor, and it is the cause of so many conversations remaining in the air:

You must determine what you want to get out of the conversation.

Whether it's the person's phone number, the reason why they are in a certain place, or perhaps convincing them to help you with this or that task, the first thing you need as a trigger for communication is a clear objective.

Why is it so important?

Imagine starting a conversation with some of the worst

"igniters" out there: talking about the weather, the government or the economy.

What are you going to get out of such an exchange? How are you going to "cut to the chase", or focus on the issue you really wanted to address?

It is uncomfortable when, during a conversation, the subject is suddenly changed to a point that was obviously the first intention.

It is much better to focus your arguments from the beginning on the topic you are investigating, and with that you will obtain two benefits: first, you will take your interlocutor by surprise (believe it or not, this is not a negative point), and on the other hand, you will not subject him/her to the uncomfortable change of topic.

Your challenge today:

Initiate a conversation with a perfect stranger (even if you are uncomfortable due to shyness), seeking to obtain concrete information. If possible, record your voice (of course, without the other person noticing it) so that later you can listen to yourself and determine what your attitude was.

(Did you sound hesitant, or determined?).

Skills you will acquire with this exercise: You will not only start to get along better; you will also learn how to get to the point in a conversation.

This will push you to develop an image of power and persuasiveness. No matter if you find it easy or difficult, you can always be more confident.

15

A QUESTION OF POWER

He who holds power is always unpopular.

- Benjamin Disraeli

In Japan they have a deep-rooted custom regarding business cards: they are considered an extension of the person and when they are offered to you, you must receive it with both hands with a bow whose intensity depends on the rank of your interlocutor.

It is as if you are being given a very valuable and delicate gift.

The problem with this excessive formality is that it is accompanied by a cold and emotionless manner, which is one of the characteristics of diplomacy. But where do we leave persuasion and power? When we are going to persuade, we cannot place ourselves "as equals" with those we are going to try to convince; we must show them that, at least from a professional point of view, we have more experience and experience in the field than they do.

If you don't think this is necessary, you must remember that an image of power is much more likely to persuade than an "ordinary" one.

Talking about business cards, and about a custom that works in any culture, is the way to take it when it is offered to you. It is best to do it with both hands, as it is proven that this way we project that we care about maintaining contact with the person.

Now, this attitude that we must develop has nothing to do with arrogance.

If you are going to sell building materials, you are not going to appear to be just another salesman; you are going to demonstrate, with your image, that you are an expert in the area; in this way you will not be selling products, but solutions (which is actually what people need when they buy something, even though most amateur salesmen do not understand this point).

Don't offer products, offer solutions.

In the West, a person of power assumes that everyone knows him or her. It may seem overbearing and self-centered, but an image of power is composed of two rather discordant ingredients: charm and remoteness.

When I talk about charm, it is the ability to please. With respect to remoteness, it is not to appear too close to the person you want to persuade, because that will detract from your professionalism. How can you send both messages at the same time?

Very simple: with a genuine smile and an impassive face.

Do a simple exercise: first cover the eyes of the smooth monkey, and try to determine the emotion expressed by her mouth. Then, do exactly the same with her eyes.

Do you notice any contradictions?

That is the great secret of this work: the combination of that smile with a thoughtful countenance.

Charming people have that magnetism that goes beyond any presentation, and that makes any superfluous formality unnecessary.

Combined with a serene countenance and moderate speed gestures, you will contribute to the expert image you need to persuade.

Your challenge today:

Learn to combine these four ingredients: a frank smile, a serene countenance without many facial expressions, manual gestures of moderate amplitude and speed, and the correct pronunciation and articulation of words in a clear tone of voice. Practice with a friend, telling an anecdote or a movie you know well.

Skills you will acquire with this exercise:

You will develop an image of professionalism, a quality that few people have in an authentic way. Even true experts in a field are sometimes insecure or taciturn when they speak. Is that what you want to project?

Remember the key word: serenity

16

HOW TO INFLUENCE BY PLAYING

Take the risk of being different, but without attracting attention.

- Paulo Coelho

If you had to choose among the most direct ways to create empathy in others, you would surely think of smiling.

What better way to show goodwill? You've talked so much about this universal gesture, you couldn't go wrong with it, could you?

There is an even more effective way to create that link: touching people. Evolutionarily, physical contact takes precedence over smiling in this respect, as touch is a sense developed many millions of years before sight (and smiling is unique to humans). When we are born, what do you think we need more: to be smiled at or to be hugged?

But so strong is the effect of touch that many people may find it uncomfortable and even offensive. Even a slight stumble usually triggers a formal "Excuse me..." So how can you use it effectively?

The key word is subtlety.

You have already studied one example of physical contact: the handshake (which, of course, merited a lesson of its own). You must add the upper arm touch to your repertoire. You will use this approach very carefully, following these guidelines: you will maintain eye contact, while calling the person by name, and you will use - mind you - only the tips of the index, middle and ring fingers, with the hand relaxed.

Why only the tips? Because you should leave only the "feel" of touching. This is especially delicate if the person's skin is uncovered. Never exert pressure with your fingers or maintain contact for more than a fraction of a second. And calling the person by name, while looking into their eyes, is crucial!

See how it's not as easy as it looked at first?

An important fact: the gesture will look terribly artificial if you do not get close enough to our interlocutor. Your arm should bend 90 degrees so that you look natural, with a slight tilt of the head towards the person.

Your challenge today:

Get close enough to someone to touch them using this procedure. Do this at least 10 times.

Skills you will acquire with this exercise:

You will develop an image of confidence while remaining formal, an indispensable condition for developing a powerfully persuasive image.

Reach out and touch; remember: very subtly.

17

THE SECRET OF THEIR EYES

Optimistic is the one who looks at your eyes; pessimistic is the one who looks at your feet.

- Gilberth Keith Chesterton

It's been less than a week since Lesson 12 when you learned how to maintain eye contact with others. I hope you haven't forgotten it, and even more... that you've practiced it!

This is the moment when you will truly dedicate yourself to observing the movements of the eyes.

You're probably thinking that I'm going to tell you what the visual, auditory, kinesthetic angles of sight are, right? I'll indulge you! If the sight is directed upwards, you are resorting to the visual memory; if it is to the sides, to the auditory; and if it is downwards to the kinesthetic. If the eyes are directed to the right side of the head, you're using creativity, and to the left memory and experience.

Happy?

The truth is that without a high-speed camera pointed directly at the face, and often watching a recording of a conversation, it is not possible to take advantage of these "quadrants", which in reality will never be entirely conclusive.

So what good are they to us in a casual conversation, I ask myself, for not only are they very difficult to pinpoint, but they also last only fractions of a second and occur one after the other without warning. And what about those that are short and quick, versus those that are long and deep? To go crazy.

For now, just focus on the way the eyes oscillate when a person is remembering a piece of information or responding to something that causes a certain emotion (such as joy or sadness).

A fun way to try this is to ask a family member or friend to try to remember what they had for dinner yesterday, and watch their eye movements. Then, ask them what their dream vacation would be like - you'll see a difference!

It is not convenient (at least at this level) that you try to be like a robot trying to determine if he looked down, to the right, etc.; it is preferable that you start associating looks with attitudes, as each person has a different way of using his eyes.

Like every lesson you have gone through, the more you practice it, the easier it will be to decipher what the person wanted to project with their gaze.

Your challenge today:

Be aware of the "style" of each person's eye movements. Some will stare at you, others... will simply wander their attention around the room. Keep in mind that these patterns are directly connected to brain programming, so you must first know how the person looks before you can draw conclusions. Remember to be very aware of their changes.

Skills you will gain from this exercise:

You will learn to determine whether a person feels engaged in what they are responding to or looks insecure. Just observing how their looks fluctuate will teach you to identify them within the overall context of conversations.

Go ahead! Forget for a moment about so many rules, quadrants and data. Just watch your eye movements carefully.

18

A WAY OF EXPRESSING YOURSELF
WHEN SPEAKING

Speaking well is an art, as is listening well.

- Epictetus of Phrygia

In a very famous research conducted at UCLA by Albert Mehrabian, it was concluded that communication is 7% verbal, 38% tone of voice and 55% gestures. These percentages seem too exaggerated to be true? And the reality is that they are not.

Mehrabian himself has explained ad nauseam that the study was based solely on isolated words devoid of any emotion (which is a **crucial** ingredient in communication) while observing only the faces of the examinees (who curiously were only women).

The fact is that this data has been presented as "absolute" over and over again in various publications, when it is not so;

but although we cannot accurately determine the percentage of each non-verbal aspect, one thing is certain: the paralanguage or tone of voice plays a very important role.

When you speak, two main centers are at work in your brain: the one that is in charge of "serving" the words on the platform for their output, and the one that actually carries out the operation of expressing them.

Let's say they ask you a really simple question: What's your name? Or they ask you about an address. The process, in this case, wouldn't be too inconvenient. But what if they ask you what you had for lunch on Wednesday of last week? In that case, the platform switchboard cannot do its job because it does not have the requested information at hand.

A third, slightly more complex scenario is when you cannot express yourself because your brain is busy thinking about the implications of your answer. In other words, if you are lying or if you are "making up a story" on the fly, you will not be able to express yourself as fluently as usual.

(Unless you have a lot of experience creating stories... or lying).

There is an even more subtle example, which occurs when the "platform" receives the information... but one of the words comes with a flaw: we don't believe in what we are saying. When we go to say it out loud, that dissonance produces a dramatic drop in the pitch of your speech. Although it is often almost imperceptible, with a little practice and some common sense it will not be difficult to detect when a word hidden in the middle of a sentence has a different volume than the others.

If you hear the phrase...

"At the meeting I was with Lopez, Rodriguez and... Fernandez."

...you will notice that there is a problem with Fernandez. Maybe he had to leave early, maybe he was too late, or maybe it's even false that he was there.

Learning to detect these voice changes has a great advantage: they are much more difficult to hide than facial expressions, manual gestures and body postures. And since they directly accompany the verbal part of the speech (which we have been used to hearing for years), it becomes easier to make a "bridge" between sound and verb in real time (without having to resort to a recording).

Your challenge today:

When you are listening to someone, try to mentally assign intonation values to the phrases he uses. Does he modulate the words correctly? How is the volume of his voice?

Skills you will acquire with this exercise:

As you begin to recognize voice characteristics, you will be able to determine volume changes in individual words.

When that happens, you'll know something strange is going on! Pay attention to what they say... and how they say it.

19

YOUR OWN IMAGE AND LIKENESS

Thoughts are like men: the better they are dressed, the better they are appreciated.

- Earl of Chesterfield

Few words arouse such disparate opinions as "fashion". Some condemn it as frivolous and others live in tune with the latest trends; but no one doubts its importance both aesthetically and economically. Managing our personal image is a fundamental skill, yet we are never taught how to do it properly.

Some go so far as to think that to "go with the fashion" is to curtail individuality.

If we define the term as a massive guideline imposed by a few experts, then I agree that it is not good to homogenize everyone's tastes. But if we go a little further and think about the term "Image", we will begin to understand a little better what we are getting at.

Why do museums go to such great lengths to present the works they display in the most spectacular way possible? If they are already famous pictures painted by brilliant artists, they should not be more careful when placing them... a Velasquez would still be a Velasquez even if it is in a poorly lit room, right?

I try to illustrate my point by letting you understand that a fundamental factor in persuasion and seduction is your appearance. I am not referring to the beauty standards that you meet or fail to meet, but to choosing the right outfit for each occasion. There we go again with the pitfall of personality: *"My image is me, I am authentic and therefore, I don't have to change anything"*. Well, I think we need an example a little more.... graphic.

Imagine two scenarios: In one, you're invited to give a speech about an innovative area in which you're an expert. In the other, it's a Sunday at the beach with your friends, where you'll be totally relaxed (thanks in part to the beer).

Would you use the same vocabulary and attitude in each case? I don't think so, and I'm sure very few people would argue with me on this statement. If you understand the difference in your verbal expression between the two scenarios, why do you think your appearance shouldn't adjust as well?

This is the reason why we see professionals who dress practically the same for any occasion. In the case of gentlemen, they choose a shirt, jeans and a sport coat for literally every scenario (except the beach, fortunately).

Do you think that if a possible promotion was at stake, you wouldn't try to make a "little effort" to dress better?

Remember that it is not about going "against your personality", or trying to look like someone you are not. It's about your image meeting certain parameters of neatness and color harmony. Although a book cannot be judged by its cover, it should definitely be spectacular enough to arouse interest in the content!

Your challenge today:

Start to be aware of the way you dress, and if possible, consult an expert in the field. As important as your attitude and your words, is the way you present yourself.

Skills you will acquire with this exercise:

Not to mention the obvious boost that a better closet can give to your motivation, taking care of your personal hygiene and appearance will give you the peace of mind and confidence you need in any situation.

Don't let your outfit distract others from what's really important: you.

20

FOCUS ON THE FACE

We are not responsible for our emotions, but we are
responsible for what we do with them.

- Jorge Bucay

The emotions we express with our faces are deeply imprinted in our genetic baggage; Paul Ekman confirmed this by going deep into the jungles of New Guinea, where there are still tribes that have not had any contact with the Western world (and still don't know about soap operas).

Through his experience with these aborigines, he was able to confirm the innate existence of seven basic emotions, namely: Joy, sadness, anger, disgust, surprise, fear and contempt.

An in-depth study of microexpressions is beyond a single lesson - even a complete volume would fall short! considering that it is possible to identify more than 10,000 different combinations among all possible facial muscle movements.

A task of such proportions takes years, even decades, even for the most dedicated researchers (Ekman himself has been studying them for 60 years and says he still has a lot to learn). How can we "mere mortals" take advantage of them in a reasonable amount of time?

The answer is simple: focusing on the most useful of all. Surprise.

Why surprise? (This is not a rhetorical question!) because if what we are interested in is to be able to pinpoint fleeting and contained emotions, we must take into account that surprise is repressed 15% to 38% more than its emotional sisters.

When we want to analyze the human face and detect micro-expressions, it is necessary to know where to look; in the graph, the white dots indicate the areas that comprise 60% of the facial expressiveness; being beginners, we should concentrate on them. With a little more experience, we can add the areas indicated by the black dots, which increase the possible combinations to 85% of the facial expression.

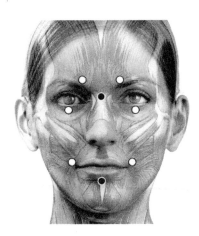

It is extremely rare for a person to hold back happiness, although it is not so difficult to remember the last time you saw someone suppress their anger. Brighter-than-normal eyes and down-turned corners of the mouth betray sadness, while the "half-smile" that accompanies contempt is classic. With disgust and fear another phenomenon occurs; they have been timed as the most fleeting of all, and unless you use a slow-motion video, it will be very difficult to appreciate them.

To detect facial movements, look at two points: The corners of the lips and the eyebrows. This is the starting point to discover them all, but don't worry if you don't succeed in your first attempts. These movements can be ultra-fast (and being overly attentive to them can cause you to lose the thread of the conversation).

Just be patient and practice whenever you can.

Want to learn how to detect microexpressions? Let's learn a little more about emotions and UAs:

Surprise is the most common of all emotions; it is also one of the easiest to detect because its displacement is very long compared to others such as anger.

Let's get started!

- AU1: Raise the inner part of the eyebrows.

This AU is one of the most difficult to fake. It is almost impossible to recreate on purpose, and only very experienced actors are able to do it at will. It is associated with: Surprise, admiration, fear, terror, and attention.

- AU2 - Raise the outer part of the eyebrows.

AU2- Elevar parte externa de las cejas

That skeptical face we make when we raise an eyebrow is usually due to the action of one or both muscles keeping the frown relaxed.

It is associated with: distrust, surprise, doubt, incredulity.

- AU5 - Lift upper eyelids

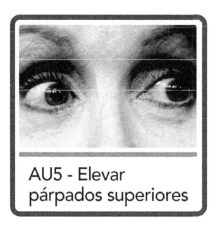

AU5 - Elevar párpados superiores

How to recognize it? We can see the white area of the eye

just above the iris. It is associated with: Surprise, interest, fear and terror.

- AU26 - Jaw drop

AU26 - Dejar caer mandíbula

The mouth does not tense; the jaw relaxes and the teeth are barely visible. This movement is rather slow, which facilitates its identification. It is associated with: Surprise, amazement, desire.

Fear, terror.

It is very common to confuse fear with surprise, since we mentally represent both in the same way: eyes and mouth wide open. But let's not fool ourselves: in fear only the inner part of the eyebrows go up, and the corners of the lips are pulled downwards.

The true ocular expression of fear is given by the combination of AU1 (raising the inner eyebrows), AU2 (raising the outer eyebrows), AU4 (lowering the inner eyebrows) and AU5 (raising the upper eyelids).

Doubts begin to arise when we see one or two AUs in full contraction and a third lags behind. In the example, we see AU1+AU2 with an intensity of 4, while AU4 has intensity 2 and AU5 intensity 1. It is a look more of sadness than fear.

Some looks may try to fake fear, but they don't have that "something" of the true emotion of horror. In this case, the struggle between AU1+AU4 is needed.

In the worst (or least credible) case, AU5 will be the protagonist while AU1+AU2+AU4 are almost non-existent. In any case, it is an expression of surprise.

Rage, anger, rage.

It is not at all pleasant to discover that someone is feeling anger, and the truth is that many times it is as easy as seeing clenched fists, a haughty tone or a louder-than-normal volume of voice.

The problem arises with disguised anger, which mainly tightens the lower eyelids and tends to tilt the head slightly forward, a remnant of when we were ready to attack our prey without warning.

- AU7: Tighten lower eyelids

AU7 - Tensar
párpados inferiores

Flexing these muscles is directly related to strong emotionality. It can be related to seduction, anger, concentration.

- AU4: Frowning

AU4 -
Fruncir el ceño.

Also known as "lowering of the inner brow area", nothing describes a frown better than a frown furrowed with vertical lines, the result of bulging fatty tissue. It is usually associated with anger, worry or sadness.

- AU23: Lip thinning

AU23 - Afinar los labios

AU23 and AU24 are the twins separated at birth. Some authors even interpret the restrained rage with either of the two; they even go so far as to interchange them freely.

In the case of AU23, the main point is the disappearance of the lips, as they flatten against each other and very important: stretching around the teeth. The good observer will notice that this will make the mouth look bigger than it is.

AU23, more than anger, is frustration; a mother who watches her child suffer the consequences of not paying attention to her, will put her mouth like this.

- AU24: Squeeze lips

AU24 - Apretar los labios

AU23's *doppelganger*, this cluster emphasizes the pressure of one lip against the other, so the mouth ends up shrinking in size, and the flesh around it will bulge enough to cast shadows just below the nose and above the chin.

AU24 is indeed a manifestation of pent-up rage.

Sadness.

Sadness is the most difficult emotion to identify at first, because it is the one we learn to hide when we are still very young. However, the need for empathy and the need to communicate to the world that we feel bad can often be stronger, and we will let it slip away for half a second.

Joy.

We have already seen, in studying the smile, that we are very bad at trying to deceive others by smiling forcibly; if the eyes are not squinted and the cheeks are tense, our expression of joy will be incomplete.

On the other hand, the micro-expression of joy will be easier to detect around the eyes, as we are more accustomed to "slowing down" our mouth.

Contempt.

Commonly confused with mirth, contempt combines a backward shake of the head (disbelief) with a half-smile that gives the expression its final meaning.

Let's look at a few more AUs, plus Behavioral Codes (BCs) descriptors (ADs) and specific movements (Ms).

- AU12: Raise commissures

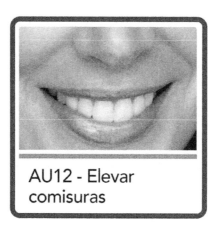

AU12 - Elevar comisuras

Raising the corners of the mouth is the clearest manifestation of joy, but it is also the most falsified of all. Never try to analyze an expression by the mouth alone.

- AU6: Tighten cheeks

AU6 - Tensar pómulos

We already know that it is an indispensable component of the smile, but we must make sure that it occurs when we notice crow's feet in the person's eyes.

- AU15: Lowering the corners

AU15 - Comisuras hacia abajo

Pulling down corners is, of course, the perfect relation to sadness; but if the person at the same time closes his eyes and pulls up a man, he is removing himself from responsibility for something, as if to say "I had nothing to do with it..."

- AUI7: Tighten chin

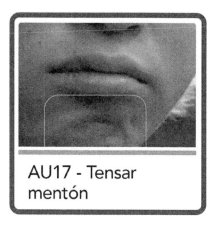

AU17 - Tensar mentón

The mentalis muscle is responsible for this bulge in our chin, and by flexing it we can feel how it stiffens. If our interlocutor does so, he or she is considering what we are saying, weighing the ideas.

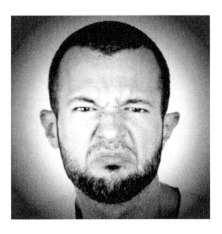

Disgust, disgust.

Disgust is confused with anger because we frown in a similar way; unlike the latter, the nose wrinkles at the septum, giving that "something smells bad" sensation.

- BC80: Swallowing

BC80 - Tragar

Mainly saliva of course, BC80 is an unmistakable sign of nervousness because when we feel nervous we salivate more than usual (even though our mouth may dry up).

- BC40: Short inhalation

BC40 - Aspirar / Inhalación corta

Rather than breathing in air, inhalation is a quick and short intake of air through the nose. It can be accompanied by a micropicor (touching the nose to conceal). It is related to hostility, incredulity, distrust, skepticism.

- M85: Nod

M85 - Asentir

As when we give a presentation or lecture and we notice the nonverbal feedback from the audience when they move their head up and down nodding, acknowledging or supporting our arguments. If the speaker does this, he or she is seeking approval.

- M64 Look down

M64 - Mirar hacia abajo

M64 occurs as a quick movement, up to one second in duration, rather than looking down for several seconds. It is related to grief, remorse, regret and insecurity in what is being expressed.

- **AD31: Jaw clenching**

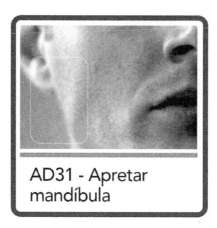

AD31 - Apretar mandíbula

A very easy descriptor to detect, we will see that the muscles of the jaw on both sides of the head tense, bulge and even the ears may move due to the tension of the adjacent tissues. It is related to anger, frustration, consternation. It usually accompanies AU24 in contained rage.

- AD45: Closing the eyes

AD45 - Cerrar
los ojos

Occurs when the eyes are closed for a second or two; not to be confused with blinking. AD45 is the desire to momentarily isolate oneself from the situation.

- AD33: Blow

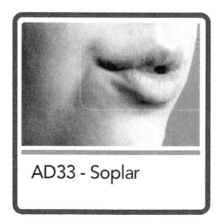

AD33 - Soplar

Even more intense than snorting, letting air escape through the mouth by momentarily inflating the cheeks is related to obstinacy, anxiety, contrariness, tiredness and dismay. It can lead to hostility.

- M60: Shaking head

M60 - Negar
con la cabeza

Although the negation with the head is apparently too obvious to be studied, what is interesting are the contradictions that arise from its appearance when the subject pretends to affirm something with the verb.

- AU9: Nose wrinkle

AU9 - Arrugar nariz

Practically the protagonist of the expression of disgust, AU9 can represent repugnance not only to food but also to situations or even people.

- AD19: Stick out your tongue

AD19 - Sacar
la lengua

This AU will be barely perceptible; most likely we will only see the tip of the tongue for less than a second and just after the person realizes that he/she expressed him/herself wrongly (inventing what he/she says, for example), and does not intend to correct him/herself.

- AD32: Lip biting

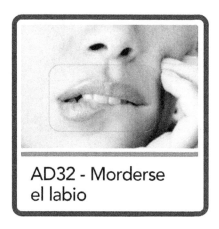

AD32 - Morderse
el labio

AD32 has a similar meaning to AD19 (stick out your

tongue), but in this case it is not necessary for the person to say a single word. By simply mentally retracting something, it can emerge. Not to be confused with the intentional bite of seduction, which is longer and more intentional.

- AD38: Dilate nostrils

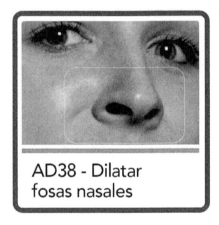

AD38 - Dilatar
fosas nasales

We can make a great effort to contain our anger and not show a hint of hostility, but even though we can control our frown and lips, a serious countenance accompanied by the dilation of the pits is a sign of anger or annoyance.

- BC82 - Shrug

BC82 - Encogerse de hombros

Sign that the subject wants to remove a responsibility or downplay the importance of what he/she is saying. It is not a shrug of several seconds and maximum intensity, it is a quick movement that usually accompanies a declaration of innocence.

- M63: Upward view

M63 - Vistazo hacia arriba

A quick glance upward is a reflection of medium- and

long-term memory when we access it. In the simplest way (without discriminating one side or the other), we relate it to remembering an event.

- AU10: Raise upper lip

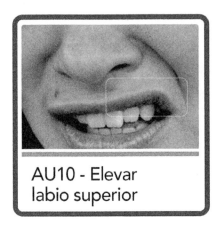

AU10 - Elevar labio superior

This is one of the most difficult clusters to locate because to detect it the face must be relaxed (when speaking it is confused with the articulation movements). Contrariness, disgust or anger are the emotions related to this AU.

- AD21: Tighten neck

AD21 - Tensar cuello

This is one of the most interesting Aus and yet, unless we have a lot of experience or an HD recording, it will be virtually impossible to differentiate from BC80 (Swallow). AU21 appears when we dissimulate terror; confirm with a suddenly pearly temple and loss of color in the face.

- **AD30:** Jaw twisting

AD30 - Torcer Mandíbula

AD30 is an almost impossible cluster to detect when the

person is speaking, and even more so when this movement is part of their baseline. If it manifests alone and without verb (to either side), it is recalling/evaluating a response. It is also related to AD19 and M64.

- M53: Chin lift

A classic power pose, you have great conviction in what you are saying at that moment. It is difficult to lie and chin up, it is only possible with a lot of practice and self-deception. It is one of the few indicators of authentic truthfulness.

- M54: Chin down

M54 - Bajar mentón

On the contrary, turning the head and bringing the chin towards the chest is mistrust, insecurity and submission. If accompanied by "Believe me", "The truth is...", "I am being sincere in telling you...", these are strong combinations of insincerity.

- M69: Head and eyes turn towards another person.

M69 - Cabeza y Ojos hacia alguien

In a group interrogation, moving only the eyes to look at a

specific person gives us a clear indication of what is going on in the speaker's mind at that moment. What he or she is saying relates directly to the person being observed; it is a matter of digging a little deeper into that relationship.

Some publications differentiate M69 into two modalities (eyes alone and head+eyes). When the head turns towards a particular person and the gaze rests on him/her, the subject is seeking his/her approval. It could be his superior or boss.

Tip: Rolling the eyes to the left (speaking from the subject's point of view, it would be in this case our right) is related to rational thinking, working memory and access to previously cataloged and processed information. Swinging the eyes to the right side , has to do on the one hand with diplomacy (you may be looking for the best words to express yourself), and in other less truthful cases, you are weighing the implications of what you are going to say (or are saying).

- M55: Tilt head to the left

M55 - Cabeza hacia su izquierda

The tilt of the head to the left side (our right) supports the interpretation given to M61 just above, only in a more subtle way. Even if we completely control our gaze, the head movement is much more instinctive and yet decipherable.

- M56: Tilt head to the right

Tilting your head to the right has similar connotations to M62, but adding a strong emotionality and empathy with what you are witnessing. You tilt your head like this when you identify emotionally with what you see.

Your challenge today:

Take a pause here. Dedicate yourself to identifying these emotions, and most importantly: whether they are true or not.

I don't remember a day that was so long!

21

DON'T TOUCH YOUR FACE

To test our nerves is to hone our skills.
- Edmund Burke

It's amazing how you can sit for a long time while waiting in a bank to apply for a loan without feeling any kind of nervousness... and the moment you start the interview with the officer, your hands start to move erratically; you wipe the sweat from your palms on your pants, you adjust a button on your shirt (which didn't need any adjustment) or you run your hand over your head or neck.

At that moment you are engaged in removing non-existent lint for the sole purpose of diverting your gaze and keeping your hands busy.

These nervous gestures are known as pacifiers, and are a special classification of the manipulators you already know.

Just as you may articulate crutches when you don't master a subject, gesturally you may be assaulted by this attitude when you lose your grip on a situation because you feel intimidated or insecure.

It's not just about touching your face, but all its variations; for example, using it as an excuse to avert your gaze, touching your neck, running your hand through your hair, scratching your nose or eyebrows... all are indications of some insecurity.

A very simple way to learn to control this situation is to become aware of your hands during a conversation.

Sounds strange, doesn't it...?

This is the only way to reduce the frequency of manipulators and feel more confident in expressing yourself.

Your challenge today:

Keep your hands away from your face (and preferably no part of your body). Even gestures referring to "yourself" should be loose. Your elbows must not, under any circumstances, touch your sides; leave them free.

They may seem like very strict rules (and in reality they

are), but you must follow them to the letter, otherwise you will appear insecure.

Skills you will acquire with this exercise:

You will get out of the bad habit of touching your face (and what you project with that gesture, such as touching or covering your mouth when you are not sure about something).

You will also learn how to use your hands to emphasize your speech.

Special difficulty for experts: I challenge you to go twenty-four hours without touching your face... Even when you're alone!

22

ZERO CROSSINGS

Not much will be done by those lacking in security.

- Thomas Stearns Eliot

I'm sure you have seen the 1984 movie "Karate Kid" and you will easily remember Mr. Miyagi, a character that won Pat Morita an Oscar. Why do I mention him in this lesson?

For a very curious reason: his style of defending himself.

What is the archetype of a martial artist about to kick the crap out of fifty opponents? Arms across the chest, legs arched, slightly sideways and maybe prancing a little.

The way Mr. Miyagi defended himself contradicted each and every one of these parameters: remember the scene when he defends the protagonist from the boys dressed as skeletons? He appeared erect; he seemed even taller, as he approached from the front and without any superfluous movement... with his arms on both sides of his body, his torso fully exposed and a serene and impassive gaze.

Personally, if I see a little old man approaching me like that, I'll assume he's more dangerous than Steven Seagal and sooner rather than later I'll take to my heels. Why is Miyagi's style so shocking? Because his trunk is fully exposed.

When we moved on all fours hundreds of thousands of years ago, our internal organs were conveniently protected from scratches, bites and claws. But when we had to stand upright to be able to move long distances, we exposed our abdomen to predators, a situation not very convenient for our survival.

This is the "standard" arm crossing, with one hand on top and one hand underneath. When someone has both hands on top, it will be difficult to change your mind. Both hands underneath can be withdrawal or pent-up anger.

How many times have you wondered about the meaning of crossing your arms? With this posture you "protect" your-self from predators, which nowadays are mostly psychological. When you feel threatened, sad, distressed or closed to other people's opinions, you cross your arms.

(It is also a very comfortable position to wait your turn at the bench).

Crossing your arms (or blocking your torso or abdomen with one or both hands, with a folder or purse, or any other accessory) affects your security image. Whether or not you feel "threatened" by these modern predators, the image you project with your torso covered is not the most suitable for negotiating and persuading.

Even in some cases where you need to be empathetic (such as convincing someone to change their attitude), it is possible that out of animosity or misgivings you may cross your arms. That will only make things more difficult.

Crossing the arms at the wrists is considered a block to communication.

Your challenge today:

Avoid this posture altogether. Remove any obstruction over your abdomen or chest when expressing yourself;

remember Mr. Miyagi and the visual impact of being "uncovered".

Skills you will acquire with this exercise:

You will look more confident, and you will leave your hands free for the respective illustrators to help you be more emphatic and convincing in your speech.

Special difficulty for experts: You will avoid crossing your arms at all costs... while still looking natural and comfortable. Sounds easy, doesn't it...?

I'm sure when you try to do it you'll touch your face!

23

IT'S YOUR TURN TO GIVE A SPEECH

Equal courage is required to stand up and speak, as it is to
sit down and listen.
- *Winston Churchill*

"That's a very difficult thing to do", "I don't know how to do it",
"I'm terrified just thinking about it". I'm terrified just thinking
about it," are some of the phrases I associate with the fear of
public speaking. At least, if it were a wild animal you could
run; from the presentation of your project to the board of
directors, you could not.

Let's face it, who hasn't suffered from stage fright at some
point?

That panic you feel is a product of your fervent need for
social approval. Human beings have a kind of internal "indi-
cator" that warns us when the situation we are facing may

have serious repercussions on our reputation or social influence. In other words, it is not the same to talk to a friend about the book you read over the weekend (slight implications), to talk to a movie actor or actress you admire (you start to get "a little" nervous) or to talk to two hundred people improvising a speech.

(Possible temporary facial paralysis).

Your body's reaction to these situations is a kind of social "allergy" that is difficult to control. Your skin feels cold, you feel a lump in your throat, your hands shake and your feet move nervously.

Could you resort to a painkiller? Maybe, but that's not the idea; there's a better way, and you've practiced it before.

It is about observation and breathing.

Remember I insisted several times that you should learn to observe? Assume a proper posture and use the corner of your eye to "scan" your surroundings. That's the first rule when giving a presentation: be aware of your audience. Some will be serious, others attentive, others perhaps a bit distant, and some even more skeptical before you begin. Your task is simple: identify the attitudes of at least 20% of the attendees.

Why do this? So that those most "in tune" with your speech serve as anchors to reassure you. In countless public speaking and stage fright guides you are invited to "fix your gaze on several people in the audience", but they don't tell you *which ones*.

At that moment you must identify those who nod their heads, those who cross their arms because they are cold, or those who are truly interested in what you are saying. Concentrate on the latter. Breathing? It is necessary to keep calm.

Aside from breathing to feel calmer, don't commit the sin of giving a lecture, class or presentation without proper practice and preparation. This is a point that has nothing to do with body language, but should never be overlooked.

Your challenge today:

Give a speech.

Do I have to give more explanations? Of course! It should be to more than 100 people. Contact a university and tell them about your interest in giving a free master class, or participating in a congress related to your professional field. They will surely agree.

Skills you will gain from this exercise:

If you have stage fright, you will begin to realize that preparation is crucial for this test. If you don't... Well, maybe you'll become a regular speaker!

Special difficulty for experts: Earn a round of applause!

24

AN INVASION OF PRIVACY

When the truth is too weak to defend itself, the only thing left is to attack.

- Bertolt Brecht

In kinesics, the study of the distance at which we interact is known as Proxemics. It comprises a series of rules, parameters and special nomenclatures for certain distances between two or more people conversing... which are of no use to you if you don't put them into practice.

In order to be able to apply it, I will simplify the description of each of the distances:

- Intimate distance starts from physical contact (Imagine a hug, for example), and extends up to 45 centimeters away.

The intimate distance is very common to use when you have to tell a secret, when you are going to deal with a very important topic or when you require total attention from the other person. In all these circumstances a strong bond of trust is required between the two of you so that it does not feel like an aggression.

You should take into account that this proximity is quite uncomfortable for most people. We can compare it to a very spicy ingredient when cooking: if you overdo it, you will surely ruin the result. In the same way, if you overdo the use of the person's intimate space, you will get the opposite result: repulsion.

To use the intimate distance correctly We stay at the limit of the personal distance (45 cm), and when we are going to say something that is directed to the benefit or welfare of the other person, let's get closer and invade that circle of trust. We should not exaggerate either...!

- The personal distance starts where the intimate distance ends, and goes up to 120 centimeters (although I prefer that you determine it by your arm fully extended forward). Not all of us are the same size, so this measurement is much more appropriate as it adapts to your size.

- The social distance starts at approximately 121 cm and ends at 360 cm; at this distance you converse with someone you don't know very well, or don't trust enough.

- The public distance, from 361 cm, is the distance you use for conferences or lectures.

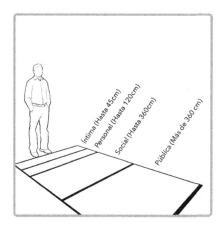

Quick tip for a meeting! What is the most powerful seat at a table? It's not the head, not the center, not the end...! It will always be the chair farthest from the front door - always hold on to that seat!

Your challenge today:

Invade a person's intimate space without provoking a negative reaction. To do this, you must choose the moment when your interlocutor is most attentive and convinced. Imagine that you want to convince him or her of something; the moment in which you release your best argument, that which you are going to say very slowly and with a voice a little lower than normal, is the precise moment to enter the intimate distance. Always remember to do it carefully and without sudden movements.

An important fact to consider: when you are about to approach, you can soften the gesture by making it a little to the side, instead of straight ahead.

Skills you will acquire with this exercise:

You will know when you have established trust with your interlocutor to the point of invading his or her circle of trust and presenting yourself as a support, a help or an unconditional ally.

Special difficulty for experts: Hold the approach for 10 seconds.

25

SPONTANEOUS GENERATION

The real friend is the one who knows everything about you
and yet is still your friend.
- *Elbert Hubbard*

When was the last time you had a spontaneous conversation with a perfect stranger? Surely you remember why it was initiated? Maybe it wasn't so "spontaneous" after all: you probably made that contact because one of you had a need at the time.

Maybe you were at the bank (definitely a great place to practice body language) and someone asked to borrow a pen. It doesn't matter how; the point is that in our daily lives, there are fewer and fewer verbal connections that originate out of nowhere, for the simple pleasure of talking.

At the level you've reached, talking to other people must

already seem not only very easy, but productive...! But you need to put a little more proactivity into it.

How would you like to start a truly spontaneous conversation? Don't worry about the topic... Well, actually, you should take it into account, since you will select it after observing the person. For example, we wouldn't talk about surfing with a chubby, gray-haired man (although we might be surprised...), so we could talk about economics, politics (Dangerous!), or better yet, history.

Have you stopped frowning? You're probably not attracted to these topics, or you wouldn't know how to start a conversation using them. Whatever, because the challenge of this lesson is not only to initiate a spontaneous conversation with a stranger, but also to learn the best way to approach a person you are going to talk to.

There are three simple rules for this, and I call it the "Triple A" technique: Attention, Action and Acceptance.

Attention is the ability of your interlocutor to stop for a moment and listen to you. Does he look too rushed trying to get to the bus stop on time? Forget it! Does he seem a little calmer and his gaze is not immersed in his cell phone? that's a good opportunity. Assess what percentage of attention you can get from the person you're going to talk to and you'll have a better chance of starting a more productive conversation.

Action is about getting the exchange going; the best way I know of is an open-ended question (that they can't answer with "Yes" or "No"). You've already chosen the topic, you know you can have their attention... now get the ball rolling.

Acceptance is a very simple rule in dialogue: Even when your opinion is categorically opposed to the other person's, avoid responding with a "no..." or a "Yes, but...", or even a "what happens is that..." as these are blockages and walls to the conversation. Instead, offer your opinion on the matter directly, without "breaking" the flow of the sentences between the two of you.

(And if you agree with what they tell you, so much the better).

Even if you put forward ideas that conflict with what you have been told, the fact that you have listened carefully and do not use verbal walls will keep the conversation flowing.

At no time do you stop applying everything you have learned so far. What points excite you? What makes you uncomfortable?

Your challenge today:

I don't have to explain, do I? Just kidding! Spark a conversation, and make it as enjoyable for both of you as you can. Do you think you can meet the three parameters above?

Skills you will gain from this exercise:

You will learn that when addressing a stranger, the way you approach him or her is more important than the topic of conversation. Having a good approach strategy, knowing how to identify the personality of your interlocutor and being able to exchange ideas in a dynamic way are persuasive skills necessary for almost any scenario that comes your way.

Special difficulty for experts: Choose a topic that is of interest only to you.

26

A SHORT PAUSE

At this point, you should already be aware of most of the postures and gestures occurring around you. The most important thing is to keep your two perceptual systems constantly working in unison.

In this image we see not only characteristics of a Beta posture but also a dissonance of attention. The woman may have her face towards us (1), but her main axis (that of the chest) is facing away from us (2). Hands in pockets (3) and feet close together (4) mark a slightly defensive attitude.

In this example we observe a defensive attitude even more marked by the right arm protecting the chest (1), and the hand in the pocket (2). As in the previous example, the feet together (3) show a certain wariness.

At first glance these two men may not agree on what they are talking about, but if you look closely their postures, gestures and eye contact are almost a mirror image of each other. This is a strong indication of rapport, so they are either on the same page or are coming to an agreement. Although gestures (3) and (2) are different, they are at the same body height, accentuating the mirroring.

A slightly more complex posture is that of this seated man; there are clues for and against both his attention and his willingness to listen. For example: with his hand he touches his chin (1) which is a classic gesture of analysis; while his right hand is firmly on the armrest (2), and could be more relaxed (his body, in general, is tense). These are the kind of signals we emit when we want to give our opinion.

On the other hand, the solar plexus is uncovered and the legs are uncrossed, so he is ready to listen. The feet slightly together are part of a beta posture; perhaps he is not so sure of what he is going to say.

In these cases (and in many others) it is recommended that you invite the person to express his or her opinion, and listen to him or her with full attention.

Another complex posture is that of this woman; the firm feet on the floor are a reflection of poise and decision; her posture and hand gesture are of attention, but at the same time she covers her genitals (possibly because of the posture of her legs).

If we were presenting a project and needed a favorable opinion (to convince others in the same group), we would ask her the question.

Finally, another strong contradiction is that of this man, who has his head in an attitude of attention (1), his elbows are relaxed on the armrests (2) but at the same time his fingers are crossed over the solar plexus and he crosses his leg, these last two points can be taken as being on the defensive (Try to put your body in this pose and you will realize that it is not very comfortable to say the least).

27

A CHANGE OF PACE

There are men whose conduct is a continuous lie.

- Baron Holbach

The tension can be cut with a knife. The air, hot and heavy, seems to fall from the only lamp in the small room, on the table where the interrogation takes place.

- "So, you were at home on Wednesday night, right?",

- "Yes! I've told you a thousand times!"

- "I see. But there's something I don't understand, didn't you tell me just a few minutes ago that you had gone out to buy beer?"

- "Uh... Well... I meant I went before I was home..."

- "But the bill for the beers was issued at 9:46 pm? Where were you before that?"

This dialogue seems to come out of a movie or police

series where they usually overdramatize these situations, but the truth is that you witness scenes like this one every day. Every time you talk to someone, you may witness verbal and non-verbal contradictions that, due to lack of training, you let go unnoticed.

Knowing how to interpret them is useful to know when a topic is uncomfortable for one or more people, when they hide information from you or even when they lie to your face.

To speak of contradictions is to speak of rhythm. The same rhythm that allows us to create music or dance, is the same term used in non-verbal communication to determine the style that each person has to communicate.

Some speak with their hands moving a lot, others are rather measured in their gestures, some speak very fast or very slow, remain with their arms crossed for hours or cannot sit still.

Diversity is the spice of life, they say; in reality what interests you is not to specify the way of expressing oneself; what is really important is to detect any visible or audible change in such expression.

When the man with the thick voice suddenly lowers his voice. Or the lady who has had her arms crossed for two days suddenly starts gesturing with her hands; or if your boss, who has always shown an iron personality, when talking to his mother on the phone, looks as if he is going to tear the skin off his face or open a hole in the floor because his leg is shaking so much.

Are they useful in lie detection? Very possibly. Are they useful in persuasion and seduction? Absolutely. Detecting a change in attitude, however small, will give you information pertinent to their mood, thoughts and feelings.

Your challenge today:

Detect changes, doubts and "holes" in the expression of others. Do you suddenly notice something different in the way they express themselves?

Skills you will acquire with this exercise:

Nothing more and nothing less than developing your ability to detect the very core of body language.

Special difficulty for experts: Can you detect rhythm changes in a perfect stranger?

28

THE ART OF SEDUCTION

The next time you try to seduce someone, avoid doing it with words at all costs.
- William Faulkner

When we hear the word "seduction", something very particular happens in us: we instantly think of an innate magnetism that certain people have who are inexplicably irresistible to the opposite sex. And although we know that appearance has less to do with this ability, those who enjoy the appellation of "seducers" have something that goes beyond simple physical attractiveness.

In fact, it has been statistically proven that the best seducers do not necessarily meet the standards of "beauty" as such (although a good facial/body symmetry helps a lot in both sexes), since the weapons used in the *Art of Casanova are* much better developed if you do not rely too much on your image.

In other words, those who know that their appearance is not worthy of the cover of a magazine, put more effort and have a greater chance of success in the process of seduction. What has been the big hurdle to overcome? As always, insecurity and fear of rejection.

There is a natural fear in everyone that they will take our advances as a joke, the "worst case scenario" being that they will laugh cruelly in front of many people (although the chances are minimal, tell me if you have not thought about it sometime).

The thing is, this fear has been exaggerated beyond reason; does it really matter if you get rejected? According to Robert Greene, more important than knowing how to seduce is knowing *who to seduce*. But although he could fill a thick volume with a "definitive guide to seduction," more than one would laugh, for no scenario is the same as another, and situations are as varied as there are people in this world.

Nor should you lose all hope: there are three key points to assimilate in this regard, and by complementing them with the non-verbal skills you have been developing, you are sure to do very well. These three factors are as follows:

Authenticity: It is said that seducers are great liars, and that they are in the habit of playing roles to "trap" their victims. FALSE: In fact, one of the conditions you must fulfill is to be authentic, not only in your intentions but also in how much you want the person.

Since we mentioned Casanova, it is pertinent to mention that this gentleman literally fell in love with each and every one of the women he seduced; and this is the only way that your words, your actions, your gestures are totally truthful.

Safety: Think about the "worst case scenario": as mentioned, being laughed at in your face and in public (if you have a worse one, welcome). Realize that no matter how bad the outcome, it's not the last person in the world - there are thousands more! And anyway, if it's cruel enough to execute that "worst case scenario", then it wasn't worth it.

Enigma: anything predictable is boring and uninteresting. On the other hand, if you show interest in her at times and the next moment you launch a contradictory message, you will make her think and ask herself, "Does she like me or not? This pondering is the most important point of the seduction process: that doubt you plant in the person is like a time bomb! Just make sure you stay close (but not too close), and move away when it is appropriate (but not for too long).

What are those signs that tell us that the other person finds us interesting? The five most important ones are: Eyes brighter than normal (because of better eye lubrication and more frequent blinking), trying to make physical contact (even if it's just brushing your hand or arm), lowering the volume of your voice a bit, and smiling (or even laughing) more than usual.

Seduction is always accompanied by a very specific sensation: well-being. The one who seduces becomes more and more self-confident, and the seduced person feels more and more attracted. But for this feedback to occur, the first step must be taken!

Of course, you have to verify that any of these signs are not a habit in the person's communication with others (which is not difficult to do, especially with smiling), which would rule it out as an indication immediately.

Your challenge today:

In the CIA they call the targets "Marks". In your case, and as a special operation, you must seduce someone. And when I say "seduce" it is in the broadest sense: convince her, through your charm, to do something you need her to do (I am not limiting it to the sexual sphere). What is the difference with persuading? Simple: in the latter you use arguments aimed at the rational part. Seduction aims exclusively at the emotional part.

Skills you will learn with this exercise:

You will manage to control your insecurity, become more self-confident and begin to understand how the emotional side of the opposite sex works.

Special difficulty for experts: I leave it to your own discretion (and responsibility).

AS IN 'MISSION IMPOSSIBLE

The man who is not afraid of truths has nothing to fear from lies.

- Thomas Jefferson

Surely at the mention of "Mission Impossible" you must have thought of its protagonist Ethan Hunt, as played by Tom Cruise. You will not be subjected to the almost implausible tests that abound in these movies, but you will demonstrate in this lesson your ability to keep your cool in extreme situations.

How will you do it? Simply by lying.

According to Paul Ekman, lies are classified in two: Creations and cover-ups. You 'create' when you deliberately make up a story to avoid responsibility, while with a cover-up you avoid disclosing information that could lead you down the same path.

At the end of the day, it's all about saving your skin.

Few lies can be considered totally black and white; they all have shades of gray, from those we tell to avoid hurting someone to those we use to deliberately hurt.

The truth is that beyond being good or bad, lies are a social lubricant. Diplomacy and politics soften, decorate and alter our attitudes, otherwise our coexistence would be unbearable. Every day we learn to keep our comments about others to ourselves to avoid upsetting the fragile balance on which our relationships are based. Lying is not the ideal way, but neither is the crude truth the best option.

I'm sure your best friend has a habit that you detest, and out of delicacy you don't express it directly. There's no problem with that, because the decision to cover up or over-look some details about others is part of the foundation of our social contract.

They say that to lie, you have to have a good memory; if you use a lie to justify your actions and leave loose ends, it won't hold up (and there are always loose ends, that's for sure).

What they don't say is that lying requires two more ingre-dients: being creative and knowing the other person well. Creativity is necessary for the details that illustrate the made-up story, and knowledge of the listener allows you to stay within the limits of the credibility that exists between the two of you.

Having said all that, the test in this lesson is a lot of fun: you will invent a character.

What can you do? Something very simple and harmless is

to play a character by interacting with a perfect stranger. You walk into a clothing store, say you are a cotton expert and want to determine the quality of the fabric of the garments.

Go ahead, make something up.

So innocent; you will have to control your attitude, tone of voice, argumentation, nerves). Forcing yourself to lie by playing a character tests all the tools you have to be convincing. You may not lie like this in the future, but this activity will enhance your credibility when you are telling the truth. Because to tell the truth with total confidence... you have to learn how to lie.

Your challenge today:

Pretend to be someone else. Even if you have a practiced script, it is possible that you will meet a fussy or suspicious person who will test your nerves. Don't despair (remember, you have nothing to lose... as long as you don't impersonate a tax official).

Skills you will acquire with this exercise:

If you are able to speak calmly by impersonating someone else, then it will be even easier for you to do so when you are yourself.

Additional difficulty for experts: Convince three strangers at the same time with your story, and with a foreign accent.

30

NETWORKING MON AMOUR

Boredom cannot exist wherever there is a gathering of good friends.

- René de Chateaubriand

Ah, the meetings. Perfect time to analyze the non-verbal communication of the attendees... and especially our own. Imagine that you are invited to a meeting, or to an event, where at the time of the toast you have 100 people in the same place (and not many acquaintances attended, or better yet imagine that you do not know anyone).

What can you do to avoid looking like an island? Well, obviously, get talking to someone. But that's too easy, you say. Of course, you say that now in lesson 29... What would you have thought a month ago? Maybe you would have been a little hesitant (and your palms would have gotten a little cold).

It's time to do something more interesting, and that is to not only start a conversation but to proactively create a conversation group among strangers. Bottom line.

The last "litmus test" is to introduce two people you have just met. Obviously you should strike up a conversation with the first one, while remaining aware of what is going on around you (women are very good at this, men have a hard time!).

This is the ultimate challenge, oriented to networking or professional link building, and to complete it you will need all the tools you have developed so far. How to recognize the interest of others, how to capture their attention, get relevant information out of them about themselves and be able to establish a link with a third party.

Your ability to perform and persuade is put to the test; don't forget to pay attention to both words and gestures.

Your challenge today:

Introduce two strangers, and engage them both in conversation. Serve not only as a listener but as a moderator. The skills you need for such a task have been thoroughly learned; it's time for your graduation. You'll know you've passed the test if you 1) introduce them, 2) have a conversation with them for at least fifteen minutes, and 3) get a reason to maintain phone or email contact.

Skills you will acquire with this exercise:

You will find that everything you have learned so far has become part of your personality.

Additional difficulty for experts: Do you really need it?

31

THE CONTROL POINT

If we are born with two eyes, two ears and only one tongue, it is because we must look and listen twice before we speak.

- Marquise de Sevigné

When non-verbal communication is studied, it is presented as a compendium of gestures, microexpressions, tones of voice, postures, techniques for observing, breathing, expressing oneself...

You are likely to feel intimidated. The amount of additional information we have to process is staggering, and to use this knowledge in a practical way, you must dispense with recordings and videos to help you interpret the smallest details.

Such a task seems almost impossible, because even with a lot of practice it is common that in the middle of a conversation, trying to detect the fleeting emotions on the person's face, while you are trying to detect the changes in the modulation of words, if they swallowed saliva when answering a particular question or if they nervously move their feet combined with micro-tapping and micro-caresses... you suddenly miss the words altogether.

Yes, I am referring to the verbal part of the speech! Is this not the structure of communication itself?

When I say "structure" I am referring to the contrast between two terms: what we want to express (with words), which is our explicit manifestation, and what we actually express (the combination with our body language), which is the combination we are looking for. Do you realize such a particular cooperation?

Just as at the beginning of our learning process you were certain that verbal communication always hid something (that "something" being the whole emotional charge of the subject), now you discover that kinesics is not complete without it.

So, will we have to become lie-detecting machines, gifted in the art of mentalism? Is it possible to have the qualities of the masters of nonverbal communication?

The answer is yes. But at a price. Let me explain with the following example: Do you think circus juggling experts learned all the feats they do at once? Of course they didn't. First they learned how to make games with some balls... then how to balance on a spinning board... then how to combine these two techniques... then by climbing a leg and balancing a tower of cups on one foot... and so on, in an additive process... with lots and lots and lots of practice.

The first 29 lessons have given you the complete journey

through the additive process of learning to master body language to become more persuasive. Maybe 30 days to master them all is too short... but rest assured that the more you practice them, simultaneously and in combination with each other, they will become a habit in you. The plasticity of the brain is impressive, you just have to put effort (and a good dose of concentration and self-motivation), and you will realize that what you have learned will come naturally and with less and less effort.

Best of all, you will enter a virtuous circle: The training will make it easier for you to apply the lessons you learn... you will feel a great satisfaction when you see that they work, so you will dedicate yourself to practice them more and more often... which will make you more and more expert. There is no secret to this, you just need to be patient and review the lessons as needed.

By the way, I was wondering: did you manage to pass all the tests in the previous chapter in "expert mode"? If so, you're on the right track. If you haven't passed them yet.... Don't forget to go back to them.

I'm sure it won't be long before you start designing your own tests, and getting better and better. Remember that it never hurts to have a progress log where you can record all your achievements in kinesics, and even test yourself against a friend who is also at your level in these studies.

WHAT MAKES THEM TICK?

Civilization is the victory of persuasion over force.

- Plato

Throughout this book I have used the term "persuasion" several times, assuming you understand what it really means; I have drawn on your prior knowledge of this convincing technique to arrive at the goal of making you more sensitive to the stimuli around you that you receive through the senses, with the ultimate goal of getting others to do exactly what you want.

But what will be the core of persuasion as such, and is there an "inexhaustible source" of it?

We often confuse terms such as manipulating, negotiating or even blackmailing with persuasion. The true definition of the latter is to convince others to do, willingly, what we suggest, without offering them anything in return. And by "nothing", I mean that it will cost us nothing, but will be of great value to our interlocutor. For example, an insurance salesman should not focus on talking about the policy as such... but about the peace of mind and security it offers.

Just when we think that we must improve the offer to attract a client, we leave the realm of persuasion and fall into negotiation. This is a crass mistake that should not be necessary, since we must first exhaust all our psychological artillery to demonstrate that the investment he is going to make, or the decision he is going to make (based on our arguments) will benefit him as much or more than ourselves.

How to do this without arousing suspicion, because any offer or offer that benefits the receiver more than the giver looks suspicious! Very simple, with a keyword I used earlier:

Solutions.

What kind of solutions? Let's ask a plastic surgeon (but one who is ethical, not a merchant). These professionals, when properly trained in their art, know that their work goes beyond surgery. Given the psychological impact that an aesthetic change will have on the patient, there are an infinite number of possible "solutions" to his or her problem. The doctor's job is to find out the real reasons that drive the person to make the decision to put themselves in his or her hands. This is not an easy task, because very seldom do we really know what we want.

This is when we come to the golden rule: If you find out what moves people, what motivates them, what drives them to act, you have everything you need to persuade them. How do you detect such motivation? If you have done all the exercises correctly so far, you will notice that people, when they speak, have different communicational "attitudes". We could roughly classify them as rational and emotional.

The rational ones are simple and not very expressive, like when we are asked questions to fill in our data in a bank form. Data such as name, address, telephone numbers... will tell us absolutely nothing about the person. But...

What happens when we ask a fishing fanatic about his last experience on the lake?

We will see a twinkle in his eyes, his tone of voice will rise and his hands will begin to dance with wide illustrators.

Do you realize what this lesson is all about? If you have already learned to provoke conversations, to identify changes of pace and to maintain your interlocutor's interest by letting him express himself, you can get to this point: to let him open up to get to his core, to discover what moves him.

Once you discover it, it's yours.

33

THE PERFECT COPY

Originality is nothing more than a judicious imitation.

- Voltaire

In his work "The Purloined Letter", Edgar Allan Poe introduces us to Auguste Dupin, a detective of the stature of Sherlock Holmes or Hercule Poirot, in a case involving the discovery of the whereabouts of a letter, stolen by a famous thief.

Despite the local police's laborious approach to such an undertaking, Dupin's ingenuity succeeds in unraveling the mystery by simply inviting the suspect to a cup of tea.

What was the technique he used? How could a simple interview determine the solution to the enigma?

Dupin pinpointed the psychology of the criminal... by imitating his face.

This theory might seem a bit "far-fetched," coming from a fictional character in a mid-19th century short story. But two researchers at Barnard College in New York discovered that there is indeed emotional *feedback* between the nerves of the face and the brain. In other words, assume a sad expression and you'll start to feel distressed; force a smile and you'll feel a little more cheerful than usual.

Without anyone noticing, try to imitate a person's face when they are talking, or simply when you see them passing by on the street.

What we are trying to look for are ambiguous expressions that could not be classified as any of the seven basic emotions. Once you do that, try to identify what you are feeling: anger? defeat? worry? elation? complacency? embarrassment? tenderness? You will see that these are feelings that are not easy to classify, but I assure you that Dupin's method will shed light on them!

34

HOW TO REACT TO A LIE

Control your emotions or they will control you.
- Zen Proverb

When it comes to body language, micro-expressions and detecting lies, few stop to think about the implications involved. I am often asked *"What should I do if I find out I am being lied to?" "I think I am being lied to, how can I be sure?" "How does it feel to know when you are being lied to?"*.

That's where I remember the central phrase of a certain superhero movie: *"With great power comes great responsibility"* And what responsibility are we talking about in this case? To take control of your emotions and keep yourself, as far as possible, out of a reaction conditioned by the moment.

Imagine for a moment that you discover (or at least suspect) that a person you trust a lot and have a strong emotional bond with is lying to you, even though he/she categorically denies it. What would your reaction be?

"It depends on the person and the lie," you're sure to reply.

A disappointment hits us very hard, and the amygdala does not think twice to run over an action that we may regret later.

The questions we should ask ourselves at that moment, regardless of how we feel inside, are the following:

- Why did he feel the need to lie?

- What is at stake?

- Why do you resort to misrepresenting the truth when you should have complete confidence in me?

Self-control is not a "switch" that we can easily flip. It requires deep daily introspection and understanding, first of all, that lying (or hiding truths) is an integral part of our psychology and the social contract in which we operate. Tact and diplomacy are related terms, yet they are not judged so harshly.

Think about that when confronted with someone who is not necessarily lying, but hiding part of the reality.

35

LET THEM ATTACK FIRST

In war, victory is based exclusively on deception.
- Sun Tzu

They say that the best defense is a well-articulated attack, but this is not always true. Most war conflicts have taught us that the best strategist is rarely the most risky; a well-planned counterattack will always be ten times more effective than the most daring attack. Why?

For one simple reason: whoever attacks is first exposed.

To retain the analogy, think of a persuasive conversation. How many times have you been besieged by those salesmen on the street presenting you with offers at point blank range? Dream vacations, credit plans or who knows what else, exposed in record time, looking to catch whoever is interested, but even a person who might be interested in the information, loses the desire to be harassed...!

This is not the best approach for a persuasive conversation, and under the concept of counterattack, your strategy from now on will be: let the other person speak and express themselves. Just like that, listen.

In Lesson 14 you learned how to trigger conversations effectively: initiate them yourself and let the other person express him/herself.

This has three benefits:

- Our interlocutor begins to exhaust his arguments: In a discussion it is normal for both people to want to speak first. What better tactic than to yield that benefit? That way you listen carefully to each and every point and opinion they want to express.

- Even if there is some kind of confusion or an issue does not seem very clear, we can invite them to explain it in depth. This will not only exhaust their arguments but also disarm them psychologically, as they will no longer be on the defensive when they see that we are totally receptive to everything they have to say.

- Your breath will run out: In an argument, you expend more energy than you realize. As the minutes go by, it becomes more and more difficult to argue; therefore, it is important to save your artillery for the end. That way it will be more devastating!

- We will have plenty of time to analyze the seven factors discussed in Lesson 11 (situation, environment, proximity, posture, gestures, volume and facial expressions).

Remember that to sustain your image of attention you must avoid crossing your arms, maintain exclusive eye contact (do not let yourself be distracted by anything or anyone) and never stop nodding your head.

When we allow others to express themselves, we also develop an image of confidence; confidence that will be reinforced by our attentive attitude and posture, the way we listen to and support others' criteria and the serenity with which we respond, will give the feeling of being in total control of the situation.

36

START LOOKING FOR LIES

Without lies, humanity would die of despair and boredom.
- Anatole France

You may wonder why I have left the lesson dedicated to lie detection almost to the end. Practically the answer comes by itself: All the techniques involved in this art require great sensitivity and dedication to study, as well as the development of skills that were dormant in you. If I had exposed them earlier, you would have been confused and frustrated, for you would not have the experience necessary to identify the subtle reactions that mark a lie.

Throughout the book, you have learned how to identify the communicational personality of others. This is more complicated than the simple "Baseline" or expressive average of a person in terms of eye movements, tics and tone of voice.

This is what is really valuable; to be able to make an approximate psychological profile of our interlocutor, even if it is the first time we see him/her, and to determine if the information he/she is giving us is true or not.

For example, imagine you go to the bank to do some paperwork. You arrive five minutes before closing time, and you ask the officer for some financial product. What would you think if you notice that the person subtly turns his eyes towards the clock, and with a mumble answers you that "The system... uhm... is deactivated at the moment".

Would you believe him?

I have given you only two factors, you have imagined them and you have already given your verdict. Do you think you needed them to be mentioned as if they were "irrefutable rules"? Even in Paul Ekman's books, the reality of this art is explained in great detail: there are no specific indications that raise a red flag and shout "Hey, he's lying! It is more a faculty of absorption, developed through active listening, surgical observation of the situation and the subject, intuition and experience.

Sound familiar?

In *Emotions Revealed*, Ekman warns how dangerous and absurd it would be to have a "recipe book" of clues about lying, such as touching the nose, clearing the throat or raising a shoulder.

Can you imagine how many innocent people could be unjustly sentenced based on these simplistic guidelines alone? The scientist categorically clarifies that it is not possible to determine a deception just by a gesture; it would be like trying to understand a paragraph by reading just one word.

You've reached a point where you have a more mature perspective of what's going on around you. Test yourself. You will see that detecting insincerity is already one of your skills.

37

THE SERENITY OF BEING IN CONTROL

> **Do not be afraid.**
> *- John Paul II*

"Come back tomorrow", *"Not available today"*, *"You are booked"*, *"You can't come in"*.

Welcome to the world of covert denials, of eternal obstacles and endless *"but..."*. To this day you put up with them playing with your time, your desire to be productive and your initiative.

It is time to put into practice everything you have learned so far, with only one purpose: to do what you want. It is time to demonstrate that you have the absolute certainty that there is nothing that can affect you, and there is no one who can hurt, harm or damage you beyond what you allow.

But you're not going to allow it, are you?

There are those who are born with the amazing power to convince others just by looking at them. I have seen them in action... it is as if the entire universe "aligned" with their desires; they show us a personality that is both devastating and charming, and it is impossible to answer them negatively or contradict them.

They always walk perfectly straight, never cross their arms and have a way of looking at you as if they were reading your thoughts (and if they do, at least they have the delicacy not to reveal it).

Don't be fooled, they are flesh and blood people like you and me, with insecurities, worries and problems; but they have understood that there is no point in externalizing those feelings (unless, of course, they are with their loved ones). This is the personality archetype that we must cultivate; the one that has no qualms about complaining about bad service, the one that has no problem talking to people to their faces, the one that does not tremble when it comes to claiming their rights.

Strangely and against all odds, these people defy Murphy's Law. While things go wrong for others (because they almost expect it, if not actually bring it about with their insecurity), they are able to "twist" luck in their favor. One wonders how they do it; and their secret can be summed up in three words:

Not to be afraid.

They are afraid of rejection, of being disliked and having their doors closed. They have realized that their rights are worth more than they had thought. How many times has a person, simply because of the inconvenience of serving us in a bank, a restaurant, a hotel or a store, has tried to "get rid" of us, as if we do not have the right to be served?

Most people prefer to avoid the conflict, back out, turn away and leave it at that... holding resentment towards the person who "blocked" you, and towards themselves for not knowing or wanting to react.

Sometimes we confuse tact with passivity, being diplomatic with being pusillanimous, being serene with being conformist. Until today you were held back. Until today, others dictated what you can do.

It is you yourself who from today onwards, whenever necessary, will claim your rights. You will make sure that your voice is heard, with total serenity and with a smile on your face, without losing your composure. You will see that you will make a great impact on others, as this attitude is not at all common.

Remember, it's your life. You must take the reins. Starting today.

38

A QUESTION OF ATTITUDE

When you can't change what you want, you better change your attitude.

- Publius Terentius

We have all at some point admired that character in real life who always makes the decisions first, always seems to be in control and even in critical moments remains impassive and cool-headed. If we had to define him, we could say that he is the *Alpha Male* of the herd, as he is in control of the situation at all times.

For obvious reasons, we will discard the term "Macho" from the expression because nowadays there is no shortage of women who have their pants on better than any of us. Either way, a contemporary "Alpha" - be it male or female - is defined by a single word:

Attitude.

And security is the precursor of attitude. A contemporary alpha does not have a harem of partners, eat first or have the best trophies (as an alpha male would in the animal kingdom). A contemporary alpha has such self-assurance that he projects it onto others at all times.

And how do you project it?

Eye contact, the correct modulation of the tone of voice, a firm handshake, correct posture, a relaxed countenance, a slight smile in any situation.

That is the best attitude.

From a very early age, we are aware that we depend to a greater or lesser extent on others. Whether they are our parents, siblings, friends or work colleagues, there is a social interconnection of dependence that conditions the way we act. And we are dependent in our daily decision making because no one likes to take responsibility for their actions, much less for the actions of others.

Where is the Alpha in all this? He is the one who seems to depend on no one; he has no worries, although we know that he has the same obligations as anyone else. Being the Alpha has nothing to do with having a high position in an organization, having lots of money or looking like he's off the cover of a modeling magazine.

Not to sound repetitive... it's a matter of attitude.

It is not being afraid to act, to speak, to decide. Are you still uncomfortable being proactive in your actions? Then understand that as long as you are, others will respect you and follow you. You will become the Alpha simply *by daring*. And that response from your environment will help you feel more self-confident, so it will be easier to have a leader's attitude. Do you realize the circle?

Learn to see the world as if the people in power depend on you, not the other way around. It's time to change the paradigm. You will not acquire exceptional skills... simply respect, and even admiration.

You already know: demonstrate an image of power... and you will have power.

39

THE ESSENTIALS TO PERSUADE

Trusting everyone is foolish, but trusting no one is neurotic clumsiness.

- Juvenal

When we speak of a "social contract" in which we human beings operate, we are referring to a tacit norm of good conduct that we have developed in the evolution of what we call civilization. It is no longer a matter of acting with sticks and stones (not even with a hidden dagger), but of acting with a universal principle in mind: goodwill.

Imagine for a moment that all human beings acted with a perpetual filter of mistrust. We would not even be able to go out on the street! This attitude would create a deep insecurity in us, because everything we do on a daily basis revolves around the relationships we establish with those around us, whether lasting or momentary.

What should be the main characteristic of such interactions?

Trust.

If the relationships we establish are currently considered a capital, trust is a very valuable asset precisely because of its scarcity. Unfortunately, we are getting more and more examples of "clashes" of this goodwill I am talking about; we have become paranoid with stories of swindles, mockery, and disdain in the economic, professional, sentimental and even family spheres.

How can we defend ourselves in such a world?

I bet you that on more than one occasion it has happened to you that a person you know little or not at all, entrusts you with a very personal problem looking for your opinion.

I'm sure you were surprised! You may have wondered: *Why not tell someone you trust more?*

This is how I want to explain this lesson to you: The trust you develop in others is one of the most powerful weapons for persuasion. When you have succeeded in "winning" a person over, it will be easier to convince him or her because your arguments will change from impositions to advice, and from advice to guidance. Gaining someone's trust is the final ingredient of persuasion... But how do you do it?

Is there a secret formula to reach this state?

The answer will make you happy: yes, there is such a formula.... And you have developed it throughout the book.

Thanks to active listening you can better interpret the needs and desires of others. You can then guide the conversation to those particular points... And show your interlocutor that you genuinely care about their problems.

When you know how to approach others and invade their inner circle, you send a message of support to their brain, which has unconsciously allowed the breakthrough without discomfort.

Finally, if you already know how to give your undivided attention, you will simply be irresistible.

Do you realize that to gain someone's trust, you practically don't have to articulate a single word?

Everything comes from **confidence;** whoever inspires more confidence will end up persuading us more easily. And if we change the point of view, you will know that you must project that same confidence to persuade.

40

NOT ONLY THAT YOU EXPECTED

Freedom does not make men happy; it simply makes them men.

- Manuel Azaña

One of the great fantastic quests of mankind has been the philosopher's stone, the secret to magically turn lead into gold. How many riches awaited those who could achieve such a feat?

Obviously, he would become the lord and master of the world...!

For centuries this legend was fed, and who knows how many apprentice alchemists racked their brains looking for the.... Compound? recipe? codex?

Although it is all (as far as we can conclude) a myth, there are rumors about a few who managed to achieve their goal.

Am I talking about turning lead into gold? Perhaps metaphorically; the nice thing about these stories is that the transmutation and transformation learned by those who achieved success was not by transforming a crude material into a valuable one.

The change was internal.

They themselves changed in the process. Whether in the end they succeeded in transmuting lead into gold is irrelevant, for whoever reached that state no longer had the slightest need to accumulate wealth and power.

I don't know if it's true or not, but if we could create gold out of nothing, I can't imagine the economic debacle that would await us.

What is really valuable is that you are about to achieve what you set out to do more than a month ago: change the way you communicate.

Surely your expectations varied between being able to persuade others, mastering the art of seduction, having an image of power or simply overcoming stage fright. I hope that at this point, you have not only understood what it takes to satisfy such longings, but that you will internalize that it was all about changing the way you think about communication.

You came here wanting to add communication tools; I hope I have not only satisfied your expectations, but also that you feel you got rid of a burden.

You have discovered in almost forty days that body language is not learned *but rediscovered*, because it was always latent in you, waiting for you to shut up your rational mind for just a moment and give your intuition a break.

It is now that you can truly be, in an authentic way, yourself. Feeling, thinking and expressing become one when you discover that you better understand those around you, and at the same time understand your inner self.

It may take you more than a day to meditate on this, but once you do... you will welcome a new stage as a human being: being able to communicate without prejudice or worries.

Take your time. When you are ready, I invite you to your last lesson.

41

ONE STEP AHEAD

A beginning never disappears; not even with an ending.
- Harry Mulisch

I never doubted that you were capable of reaching this point. Despite the obstacles imposed on the journey, I knew that your excitement to learn would not be extinguished halfway; rather, it would become a passionate fire to discover, one by one, the lessons I was inviting you to learn.

I trust that your discipline helped you to follow the order and to stick to each exercise. If it didn't... remember you can always go back a few steps.

There is no rush.

Your apprenticeship does not end here. The process has taken little more than forty days, but you must remember the dozens of years you have faced a hostile world. Do not put this book aside like any other. Whenever you want, review any of the lessons, remember how you did in each exercise and try to improve yourself.

The last lesson is about your responsibility; to keep communicating better every day, and understanding that no human being is perfect. Each and every one of us makes mistakes, we are insecure in one or more aspects and thousands of times we have been frustrated by not being able to express ourselves or make ourselves understood as we wanted to.

You have a great responsibility: to help me help us all continue learning. That was the germ that started this movement a few years ago, and it has materialized in this book as a stepping stone.

I invite you to help others become aware of body language to better understand each other... and ourselves.

Thank you for joining me on this journey, I bid you farewell and hope to see you again soon!

Jesus.

Printed in Great Britain
by Amazon

76194387R00129